PRAISE FOR GREEN CHIC

"Appealing to readers' sense of style, Matheson slyly steers us toward consumer goods and services that minimize our earth-stomping human footprint. She's brave enough to say 'buy less of everything,' and even the politically fraught 'buy nothing.' Matheson's genius is to make this seem not only doable, but fun."

—Elizabeth Royte, author of *Garbage Land: On the Secret Trail of Trash* and *Bottlemania: How Water Went On Sale and Why We Bought It*

"*Green Chic* is a bible for any environmentally-conscious fashion-phile—from a green dry clean to a pure pedicure, Matheson serves up style in a life guide to saving the planet and looking good doing it!"

—Jill Kargman, author of *Momzillas*

dear Cathy,
thanks for helping to
save the earth...
in style!
♡Christie

green chic
SAVING THE EARTH *in style*

Christie Matheson

SOURCEBOOKS, INC.®
NAPERVILLE, ILLINOIS

Published by Sourcebooks, Inc.
P.O. Box 4410, Naperville, Illinois 60567-4410
(630) 961-3900
Fax: (630) 961-2168
www.sourcebooks.com

Library of Congress Cataloging-in-Publication Data

Matheson, Christie.
  Green chic : saving the Earth in style / Christie Matheson.
    p. cm.
  Includes index.
  ISBN-13: 978-1-4022-1082-2 (trade pbk.)
  ISBN-10: 1-4022-1082-5 (trade pbk.)
  1. Environmental responsibility. 2. Alternative lifestyles. 3. Organic living. 4. Sustain-
able living. 5. Environmentalism. I. Title.

GE195.7.M38 2008
333.72--dc22

                            2007044209

                    Printed and bound in Canada.
                    WC 10 9 8 7 6 5 4 3 2

To my sister, Jen

"It's a question of discipline," the little prince told me later on. "When you've finished washing and dressing each morning, you must tend your planet."

—Antoine de Saint-Exupery, in *The Little Prince*

CONTENTS

INTRODUCTION

I am not a veteran environmentalist. I don't live in a house made of recycled tires, I've never handcuffed myself to a tree, and I don't grow my own organic rutabaga. But I *am* interested in being green. If you picked up this book, the same probably applies to you.

I'm a writer. I write about food and wine and fashion and spas. I've written about how to make a cake that looks like a designer handbag (you would not believe how long that takes), what goes into a perfect martini, and the thread counts of certain Italian sheets. In other words, I often write about things that are considered chic. (Does that mean I am chic? Well. You make the call in a few chapters.)

I'm a regular person, and I enjoy certain creature comforts: I like taking hot showers. I don't want to convert my entire wardrobe to hemp (though I did find a sexy hemp-and-silk top that gets tons of compliments). I'm never going to be someone who can go for a whole year without buying anything new. But that doesn't mean I have to abandon any hope of green living. While researching this book—which I did for a year while living half the time in Boston and half the time in San Francisco, where my boyfriend, Will, lives (he's now my fiancé—I'll tell you later about how he proposed with an ecofriendly ring)—I discovered that you can definitely be green without giving up everything you love. I also figured out that being green can be decidedly chic, a combination that no other green living book has explored.

It's a no-brainer. None of the designer cakes, martinis, or Italian sheets are even remotely as chic—and I mean really, truly, deeply, timelessly, Jackie-O-and-Audrey-Hepburn chic— as living green.

This is not because being green is trendy right now and a current pet cause of many celebrities (though it is, of course, and that helps raise awareness about a hugely important issue). Fads come and go—if you look at a photo of yourself decked out in your middle school style (what was *up* with those bangs?) you'll appreciate that—but ecofriendly living is more than a passing phase. Like anything truly chic, it is always in style. It *has* to be. Green living needs to become the standard, so that at some point we don't even label it anymore.

In order for that to happen, we need to embrace the fabulousness of green living. And it *is* fabulous. Being green can help you look gorgeous, have a killer wardrobe, feel amazing, travel in style, create a home that's an oasis, host fun parties, eat incredible food, and drink phenomenal wine, all while feeling more connected to your friends, family, and nature. Yeah, okay, this all sounds like a commercial for green living, but I'm not kidding. If you don't believe me now, talk to me in 212 pages. This book gives you all kinds of easy ways to be green—and to be chicer than ever at the same time.

And anyway, all the chic stuff is just a very nice bonus. Which brings me to the real reasons *why* living green is the only way to go. I'm going to get serious for a minute. I promise the rest of the book isn't this stern and scary. But before we get to the fun ideas we need to *get* why it's important to live green.

We are destroying our planet.

Does that sound too dramatic? This is a dramatic situation. You probably hear about this all the time, and maybe you're tempted to tune it out, but here's the deal: Human activity—burning fossil fuels (oil, natural gas, and coal) to power our cars and airplanes and energy plants and the factories that make all the stuff we consume like crazy, plus cutting down trees in an out-of-control way—is causing the release of way, way, way too many greenhouse gases (carbon dioxide [CO_2], methane, and nitrous oxide) into the atmosphere. (Since CO_2 accounts for about 80 percent of greenhouse gases, that's the one you usually hear about.)

Those excess greenhouse gases are trapping heat close to the earth's surface and warming up the atmosphere and oceans. Dangerously so. Glaciers are melting. Deadly heat waves are becoming increasingly frequent. Catastrophic hurricanes are raging more often. Cities are flooding, while lakes are drying up. Farms and our food supply may be threatened by drought. Destructive wildfires are escalating. Polar bears are drowning. Penguins are dying. This is bad.

And that's what's happening now. The consequences in a few decades could be far more painful. Billions of people without drinking water. Entire cities gone. Thousands of species wiped out, and other species moved to new regions where populations can't handle the diseases they carry. Major illness epidemics.

Just because you can't *see* global warming every day in your neighborhood in the way that you might see the effects of an earthquake or flooding or fires or a terrorist attack doesn't mean it isn't real. It's real, and it's devastating.

And global warming isn't the only environmental disaster created by human activity. What we do also pollutes the air, not just with dirt and dust, but with poisonous fumes. We're polluting water and soil, too, and putting nasty chemicals in our mouths and all over our bodies. We're making the air inside our homes even more toxic than the air outside. We're wasting our limited supply of water. We're using up nonrenewable resources, like petroleum, and fighting insane wars over them.

Note: Focusing mainly on stopping global warming—and even more specifically on reducing CO_2 emissions—is perhaps an oversimplification of the situation, but if we take care of that, we'll go a long way toward solving the other issues as well. In this book there is definitely an emphasis on ways to cut your personal CO_2 emissions—but I explain ways to address a lot of the other problems, too.

We need to start immediately. There is time—barely—to stop destroying the planet before the mess we've made is irreversible. So let's do it.

You might be wondering whether living a chic green lifestyle can really make a difference to the state of the earth and the health of those of us living here.

It can.

True, buying an ecofriendly cashmere sweater or a lipstick in biodegradable packaging will not stop global warming, create more sources of clean water, or get rid of the toxins damaging the planet (and the people on it). But changing our mindsets about the way we live, seriously reducing our individual contributions to global warming (thereby making dramatic changes as communities and as a nation), and using our power as consumers to encourage systemic change can quite literally save the world. Whew. How's *that* for making a difference?

What's more, acquiring a greener mindset means acquiring less: less stuff, less clutter, less mess, less stress. It's a calmer, more relaxed, more fabulous way of living that's about quality (of products, yes, but also experience and connection to nature and those around you), not quantity. And that is chic, indeed.

Green Chic is not an exhaustive guide to every aspect of green living (because then it would be a really huge book!). I decided instead to address things *everyone* can do, even if you don't own a home, aren't planning renovations, and can't set up systems that enable you to live off alternative energies such as wind or solar power.

Making such major changes, like installing solar panels or doing a completely green home renovation, are fantastic ways to be green—see page 198 to learn about good sources of information on those topics. But this book is all about simple, easily attainable, and, of course, *chic* green things to try.

Lots of environmental tips (including some of mine!) push limiting, cutting back, and narrowing the universe of products you should use and things you should do. And though right now that has to be part of being green, it's also about shifting your thinking and understanding why being green is so good for you, for everyone around you, and for the planet. It's not about depriving yourself, it's about—sorry, this is going to sound really touchy-feely—living in a positive way for the world around you. It's not just about what you can't do, but what you *can* do to effect change.

No, you can't buy your way into being green. But when you do buy things, you can make positively green (and chic) choices.

Why read what I have to say about all this? When the environment started becoming a hot topic a couple of years ago, I wanted to jump on the bandwagon and learn *how* to live a greener life and *why* the things I could do actually made a difference.

I wasn't planning to write a book—I just began reading. I read eco-advice books written by people who actually do live in homes made of recycled tires (not happening in my life anytime soon), and I read a lot of books and articles that either glossed over the *why* part, or didn't give me enough of the *how* part. And though some books make quips about the fact that green living can be stylish, they don't back that up with evidence. I couldn't find a book or magazine article that explained to me, in a satisfying way, how I could be green and chic. (Yes, lately there have been countless magazine articles telling you about the things you can do to go green—at this point I've written a lot of them. But very few of them are allotted the page space to go deep enough to render a thorough understanding of going green. Many of them suggest products and services that might look green but that aren't *really* green.)

So I decided to start researching (and researching, and researching) and trying a zillion different things so I would know what works, what the point is, and what's both green and chic. *Green Chic* shares what I learned along the way, all of which has helped me to become much greener, even though I'm still not pristinely green. (And that's okay—you don't have to be. But we all need to do everything we can.) This is an exciting time to be going green—the information and products and innovative ecofriendly designs out there are better than ever, and they are getting more widely available every day. *Green Chic* offers guidance—and, hopefully, a little entertainment—for anyone who wants to live greener, and do it with style.

P.S. It may have occurred to you that a book is not the ecofriendliest of items. You are correct. But I think spreading this message is worth it. And *Green Chic* is printed on 100 percent post-consumer waste recycled paper (Ancient Forest Friendly (AFF) and Forest Stewardship Council (FSC) certified; see the first page of the book for details), using vegetable-based ink. Also, I'm donating 50 percent of any royalties it earns (after taxes) to environmental organizations including the Alliance for Climate Protection (climateprotect.org), Roots & Shoots (rootsandshoots.org), and the Central Park Conservancy (centralparknyc.org).

Chapter One

GREEN GLOSSARY

Here are brief definitions for some frequently used environmental terms. I didn't *really* know what a lot of these meant when I started this project. Gaining an understanding of their meanings can help the concepts of green living make a little more sense. I explain many other terms in context throughout the book; in this section I've attempted to cover the basics to get you started. If you already know these, feel free to skip ahead. They'll be here for you if you need them.

Alternative energy: Environmentally friendly, sustainable energy not derived from burning fossil fuels—wind and solar energy are two examples.

Biodegradable: Made primarily of natural components and able to break down and be absorbed into an ecosystem.

Biodynamic: A rigorous form of organic farming that uses specific field and compost preparations according to an astrological calendar. Biodynamic farms are certified by the organization Demeter.

Carbon dioxide: (CO_2) emissions A common way to quantify an individual's or household's impact on global warming. Burning fossil fuels such as petroleum, coal, and natural gas emits CO_2, which is also a naturally occurring greenhouse gas, into the atmosphere. Because of human-related emissions, the level of CO_2 has gone from about 280 parts per million (where it was before the industrial era began) to more than 350 parts per million—and increasing quickly—today. The average American is responsible for about 22 tons of CO_2 emissions per year. Personal activity (as opposed to industrial activity) accounts for more than 30 percent of all CO_2 emissions in the United States.

Carbon neutral: Describes an entity (or person) that has effectively neutralized the impact of the greenhouse gas emissions caused by its (or her) activities, so there is no net contribution to global warming.

Climate change: A widespread change in weather patterns or temperature.

Compost: To let organic waste break down and decompose into a mineral-rich material that can be used as mulch or to enrich soil for gardening.

Dioxins: Chemical by-products from the manufacturing of synthetic chemicals and the incineration of chemical-containing products. They are powerful carcinogens that also disrupt the endocrine system, damage the immune system, and cause kidney and liver problems and birth defects.

Energy Star: This Environmental Protection Agency (EPA) program evaluates the energy efficiency of home appliances and electronics. Energy Star–rated products are generally significantly more efficient than their non–Energy Star counterparts.

Factory farm: A concentrated animal feeding operation (sometimes called a CAFO) with one thousand or more head of livestock.

Food miles: The number of miles food has traveled from where it was produced to your plate. Food in most U.S. grocery stores has traveled an average of about 1,500 miles.

Formaldehyde: A chemical used as a preservative in beauty products as well as in paper products and wood furniture. Formaldehyde is emitted from these products as a gas. It's a known carcinogen and an irritant to the eyes, nose, throat, and respiratory tract.

Fossil fuels: Fuels such as petroleum, natural gas, and coal that come from decomposed fossilized plants and animals.

Global warming: An increase in the average temperature of the air near the earth's surface and the oceans. It's caused by excessive greenhouse gases, such as carbon dioxide (CO_2), being released into the atmosphere and acting as a blanket to hold the heat close to the earth.

Greenhouse gases: Gases that trap heat in the earth's atmosphere. Carbon dioxide (CO_2) is the most prevalent greenhouse gas; methane, nitrous oxide, and fluorinated gases are others.

Greenwashing: When corporations and products claim to be environmentally friendly—but those claims are suspect.

Kilowatt-hour (kWh): A unit of energy equal to 1,000 watt-hours. A watt-hour is the energy used for a 1-watt load to draw power for 1 hour. You can calculate kWh by multiplying the wattage of a device (such as a hair dryer or a lightbulb), multiplying it by the hours used per day, and dividing it by 1,000. Using 1 kWh results in the emission of about 1.5 pounds of CO_2.

Organic: When referring to food or food ingredients, organic means something that has been grown without the use of synthetic chemical pesticides or fertilizers. To be labeled organic in the United States, a food needs to meet stringent USDA requirements. Beauty products labeled organic are not subject to the same guidelines. More generally, organic refers to matter that was recently living and is able to decay or decompose.

Parabens: A group of chemical preservatives used in many beauty products. They mimic the effect of estrogen and may be carcinogens.

Petroleum: Also known as crude oil, petroleum is a naturally occurring liquid fossil fuel. It is a major energy source and a raw material used to make plastics, fertilizers, and pesticides. It is a nonrenewable resource (in other words, there's a finite supply in the world).

Phthalates: Industrial chemicals that are frequently added to consumer products, generally to act as plasticizers (i.e., to make plastic flexible) or as solvents to make fragrances last longer. In the personal care realm, they are often found in nail polish, makeup, and hairspray. Phthalates are suspected carcinogens and hormone disruptors that can enter human bodies via inhalation, skin absorption, and ingestion.

Postconsumer waste: Material that has been used by the consumer and discarded (or recycled).

Recycling: Processing used materials into new raw materials.

Volatile organic compounds: (VOCs) VOCs are chemical compounds emitted as gases from some solids and liquids at room temperature (they don't need to be superheated or frozen or anything). Many conventional paints, lacquers, cleaning products, cosmetics, wood preservatives used on household furniture, and dry cleaning chemicals give off VOCs. So do gasoline, motor oil, and kerosene. VOCs can cause headaches; eye, throat, and skin irritation; nausea; and kidney and liver damage. They may also be carcinogenic and harmful to the central nervous system.

Chapter Two

LITTLE GREEN THINGS

Change is hard. It can be uncomfortable and unsettling. Cases in point: Moving. Breaking up. The first few days with a new haircut.

But the change to a greener way of stylish living—and a green chic mindset—is worth making. Luckily, the change doesn't have to happen all at once. There are many easy, utterly painless things you can do that make a real difference. That's what this chapter is all about. As you ease into these little green habits, I suspect you will slowly but surely begin to shift your awareness and realize many other little green things you could be doing. It gets kind of addictive, and it's fun.

For now, even if you aren't ready to dive into the suggestions in the rest of the book yet, try one or two (or hey, all) of the ideas in this section. They're easy, and they don't cost a thing. Actually, that's not true. A couple of them do cost something, sort of. (But just a bit, and they'll ultimately end up saving you money.) You may have heard of some of these before, but read on—knowing *why* it's helpful to do these things (and knowing what chic things you can use to make the changes) makes greening your life even easier.

Ready to start getting green?

CHANGE A LIGHTBULB

Switch out one incandescent—that's your basic lightbulb—for an energy-saving compact fluorescent lightbulb (CFL), which you can use in most regular lamps.

Energy Star–rated CFLs use about two-thirds less electricity than incandescent bulbs. That's because 90 percent of the energy an incandescent bulb generates is converted into heat, not light— so that energy is wasted (and damn, you can scorch yourself by accidentally touching an incandescent that's been on for a while).

Making the switch to a CFL in just one lamp that's on for four hours a day will reduce your annual carbon emissions by around 150 pounds. If every household in the U.S. did it, that would save as much energy as it takes to light 2.5 million homes per year and equal the effect, in terms of greenhouse gas emissions, of taking 800,000 cars off the road. In general, electricity use is a key area for making changes: It's the biggest source of carbon emissions in the U.S., accounting for 39 percent of all carbon emissions.

Emissions explained

With information on going green almost everywhere in the media these days, you've probably heard something about emissions—

and about how we all need to reduce said emissions. I didn't know quite what that meant when I started researching this book, so in case you're still wondering, here's the scoop: *Emissions* refers to the carbon dioxide (CO_2) and other greenhouse gases released into the atmosphere when fossil fuels such as petroleum, coal, and natural gas are burned. You may be thinking that the only time you actually burn fossil fuels is when you drive, but in effect you're burning them when, for example, you use energy from a power plant to dry your hair or heat your water, or when you use a product (whether it's a poufy new dress or a tiny new cell phone) that requires fossil fuel energy to produce. So we're pretty much constantly kicking out emissions. In fact, human-related emissions have caused the level of CO_2 (and other greenhouse gases; see page 4) in the atmosphere to go from about 280 parts per million (where it was before the industrial era began) to more than 350 parts per million now—and that number keeps going up. All the extra stuff in the environment means heat is getting trapped on earth, and voila: global warming. Each American is responsible for about 22 tons of CO_2 emissions per year, on average. So reducing your personal emissions means saving *tons* of CO_2 from entering the atmosphere.

Finding CFLs is getting easier, but they still aren't available at every drugstore and supermarket—I can't always find them in those places. I buy my CFLs at the local hardware store, which, it turns out, is also a brilliant source for mason jars and other affordable, safely reusable glass containers.) You can also find CFLs at Home Depot (homedepot.com) and at green home stores.

When choosing CFLs, be aware of the wattage and the color (denoted by the Kelvin temperature). The first time I bought one, I didn't know what wattage or color to look for, and I ended up with a living room light that was way too bright and way too blue. It also had that rather unattractive coil. (Will doesn't tend to notice when I change things in our house, but he vetoed that bulb immediately.) I figured that was just the deal with CFLs, and I almost gave up on them. I'm glad I didn't, because not all CFLs are created equal.

First of all, you can now easily find CFLs that look a lot like regular bulbs. No coil. As for the brightness, keep in mind that a 20-watt CFL is roughly equivalent in light output to a 75-watt incandescent bulb. Twenty CFL watts is too bright if you're going for flattering ambience, but it'll work in the bathroom, where you want to be able to see clearly. In my living room I now have 13-watt CFLs. To get the right color, check out the Kelvin temperature of the CFL. Lower Kelvin temperatures (3,000 degrees and under) give warm light; higher Kelvin temperatures (especially in the above-6,000-degree range) give much cooler, bluer light. The 13-watt bulbs in my living room are 2700 Kelvin, and in the kitchen, where I want brighter light, I have a 19-watt, 2700 Kelvin bulb.

A note on cost: When you go to buy a CFL, be prepared for sticker shock—they are pricier than incandescent bulbs. One CFL might run you $4 to $7—ten or more times as much as an incandescent. But it will last up to ten times as long—the average lifespan of a CFL is five years—meaning you have to buy far fewer bulbs, *and* it should save you more than $30 in electricity costs over the bulb's lifetime. Which means you're actually saving money.

Tip: Turning it on for the first time? Remember that CFLs take a little while (usually thirty seconds or so) to warm up to full intensity, so don't worry if it seems dim at first. It will get there. Speaking of dim, CFLs don't work yet in lights with dimmer switches. So don't use CFLs and dimmer switches together.

CFL suggestions

Room: Your bathroom
Wattage: 23
Kelvin temperature: 3000
Why: If you want to look gorgeous, you gotta be able to see *everything* in there.

Room: Guest bathroom
Wattage: 19
Kelvin temperature: 2700
Why: Ample but flattering light means friends won't hate using your bathroom.

Room: Kitchen
Wattage: 19
Kelvin temperature: 2700
Why: You want to see clearly—but not be caught in the glare if people are gathered around.

Room: Living room
Wattage: 13
Kelvin temperature: 2700
Why: This is bright enough for reading and keeping you awake till
Entourage comes on, but still lovely and inviting.

Room: Bedroom
Wattage: 11 to 13
Kelvin temperature: 1500–2700
Why: Go for the lower wattage and temp if you want to evoke
candlelight in your boudoir—if you're a lights-on kind of gal,
try something a little brighter.

When a CFL does burn out: CFLs last a long time, but
they don't last forever. When they do die, don't toss them in the
trash. They contain a small amount (about 5 milligrams or less)
of mercury, a neurotoxin. That's not a huge amount—older
home thermometers contain about 500 milligrams—but if you
throw out a CFL and it breaks, the mercury could seep into soil
and groundwater or evaporate into a toxic gas.

However, it turns out that much mercury is still *less* than
the amount released into the atmosphere by an incandescent
bulb. (Because incandescents draw so much energy, and because
electricity plants are one of the biggest environmental mercury
contributors around, operating an incandescent emits about 10
milligrams of mercury over the life of the bulb.)

But you should still recycle the CFL or dispose of it properly. And there's the rub. Unfortunately, you can't just toss it in your recycle bin. Check earth911.org or lamprecycle.org to find out about recycling and disposal options near you, or take it to a local hazardous waste disposal site. Or drop it off next time you're shopping at IKEA—they offer a CFL take-back program and recycle them safely. As a *last* resort, seal a burned out CFL in two plastic zipper bags before disposing of it so if it does break the mercury won't seep into the atmosphere. Be sure not to dump it in an incinerator.

FLIP THE SWITCH

No matter what kind of bulbs are in your lamps, turn them off when you leave the room. Depending on how many lights you tend to leave blazing and for how long, this could save a serious chunk of energy—and cash on your monthly electric bill.

For argument's sake (a very conservative argument), let's say you've got a lamp with a 75-watt incandescent bulb that you haven't gotten around to changing to a CFL yet. Maybe it's a lamp in your entryway that you turn on right when you get home at night—then leave on for three hours even though you're not spending any time in your entryway. Shutting it off right after you've left the entryway would keep about 125 pounds of CO_2 per year out of the environment. That's *one* lamp. If you have a habit of leaving on more than one, or every light in the house, or any lights for more than a few hours at a time—all day or all night or the whole week you're on vacation—well, you do the math.

This is about as easy as a change gets. All it takes is a little movement of the wrist (okay, maybe a finger, too), and once you get in the habit, it becomes second nature. I found that when I realized how much energy lights could waste (and, hence, how much needless CO_2 was being emitted when I left lights on), I was able to change my ways quickly. I did enjoy being welcomed to my apartment by the warmly glowing lamp on my console table that I would leave on *all day*, but those few seconds of illumination just aren't worth the energy. Now I get home, and *then* turn on the light. Brilliant, yes?

Atmosphere advice: If you're listening to music or watching a movie or eating dinner, and you don't need lights to read or work or do delicate embroidery work (you do that, right?), shut them off and light some candles (non–petroleum-based ones; I explain why on page 50) and see what a treat that is. You deserve candlelight every night.

SIP FROM THE TAP

Instead of toting around bottled water, fill up your own reusable water bottle with regular or filtered tap water and quench your thirst with that. As a former bottled water junkie, I know how crazy this idea might sound, but there are many reasons why bottled water is not a green chic accessory.

The bottles themselves are most often made from plastic polyethylene terephthalate (PET), which is derived from petroleum, a nonrenewable resource. Producing one kilogram (2.2 pounds) of PET requires about 40 pounds of water and emits more than five pounds of carbon dioxide (plus sulfur oxide, carbon monoxide, and nitrogen oxide) into the air. Once the bottles are made and used, only about 20 percent of them are recycled—the rest end up being littered or incinerated or dumped into landfills. In the United States (home to the some of the safest drinking water on the planet) we go through about seventy million water bottles a day.

And the water *in* the bottles isn't necessarily better than tap water. About 25 percent (or more) of bottled water actually *is* tap water. Really, really expensive tap water: We spend up to ten thousand times as much per gallon on bottled water as we do on tap water. Do you know what other fabulous things you could be spending that money on?

Because bottled water is much less strictly regulated than U.S. tap water, it's more likely to be contaminated with bacteria or to contain traces of carcinogenic chemicals. If you prefer the taste of bottled water or worry about the quality of water in your area, filter your tap water. The up-front cost for a filter is more than the cost for one bottle of water, yes, but it'll save you serious cash over time.

Oh, and don't just buy one disposable plastic bottle of water and keep reusing it. Typical disposable water bottles have a very narrow mouth and are tough to clean, so they may harbor bacteria. Studies have shown that disposable plastic bottles may also leach potentially carcinogenic chemicals such as phthalates into your water over time. Plus, ratty old plastic water bottles aren't very cute.

Glass and stainless steel are the healthiest choices for reusable water bottles. Glass isn't as practical to lug around, but

I used my conversion from bottled to tap water as an excuse to buy a beautiful Simon Pearce (simonpearce.com) glass pitcher I'd been ogling—I fill it and chill it in my fridge. Sigg (mysigg.com) makes fantastic aluminum bottles with nontoxic, non-leaching liners that come in a variety of sassy colors and patterns. Kleen Kanteen (kleenkanteen.com) makes subtle silver stainless bottles in sizes from 12 to 40 ounces. REI (rei.com) carries both brands. And it turns out that those classic stainless steel L.L. Bean (llbean.com) thermoses that my mom used to fill with hot Tang are still a great idea for beverages on the go, especially if you want yours to stay hot or cold. So retro, so cool.

Tip: When you're thirsty, and you don't have your safe and trusty reusable container, you may occasionally need to buy bottled water. If a glass bottle is available, choose that over plastic—manufacturing a plastic bottle produces one hundred times the toxic emissions that manufacturing a glass bottle does. It's also better to reuse in a pinch, because glass doesn't leach harmful chemicals into your water the way plastic can (though it's still not easy to clean, and bacteria may start to breed if you keep using it). Whatever you use, when you're done with the disposable, don't toss it. Recycle it. You might even get a nickel back.

Just one cup

No, I'm not going to tell you to cut back on coffee—that would be mean. But while we're on the subject of reusable beverage containers, let's address coffee cups. If you're a frequent purchaser of coffee by the cup (or tea, or jumbo frappi-whatevers), get in the BYO habit. As in bring your own safely reusable coffee cup (in stainless steel or #2 or #5 plastic—for more about the seven common kinds of consumer plastic, see page 42) instead of using a new disposable cup every day. In the United States we use about fourteen billion disposable paper coffee cups and twenty-five billion Styrofoam coffee cups each year. If you use one coffee cup every day for a year, you're generating about 23 pounds of waste. Because paper coffee cups are generally lined with (petroleum-derived) plastic, they can't easily or safely be recycled, and they won't readily biodegrade in a landfill. Styrofoam cups are made from the plastic polystyrene (that's the #6 plastic—again, for more on plastics, see page 42), which is difficult to recycle, requires a lot of energy to produce, and has been shown to leach styrene into foods and liquids. Styrene is a potential carcinogen and hormone disruptor. Who needs that first thing in the morning?

For more about the coffee *in* your cup, check out page 79. (Don't worry. I'm not going to tell you to quit caffeine there, either.)

WASTE LESS WATER 🐟

Keep the faucet running for as short a time as possible every time you need H_2O. The average faucet runs through three gallons of water per minute. So if you leave it on while you're brushing for the dentist-recommended two minutes, twice per day, that's 12 gallons a day—4,380 gallons per year—going literally down the drain. This isn't just about conserving the actual water, though I'll get to that in a second. Getting all that water ready for you and re-treating it after you've used it (which usually happens at a publicly-owned water treatment facility) takes energy. Between pre- and post-treatment, those 4,380 gallons that you didn't need to use send almost 25 pounds of CO_2 into the environment. And that's just when you're brushing your teeth.

An easy way to cut back on water use is—get ready for some earth-shattering advice—to shut the water off while you're brushing your teeth. As you get into water-conserving mode, try to keep the faucet off as much as possible at other times—while you're washing dishes or cleaning your bathroom—and don't let the water run for five minutes before you get in the shower. (For more about ecosavvy showers, read on in this chapter.)

There are probably other times you let the water run needlessly, too. For example (this is a little embarrassing): When I do a "number two" and there are people in the next room, I turn on the faucet. This creates a nice little noise barrier and makes me feel like I have privacy. (Sorry to bring up the topic, but hey, we all need to do our business. Sigh. I guess I don't need to do it while wasting gallons of water.)

Conserving water might sound like advice you've heard before—my grandmother used to tell me this all the time—but by following it now you're actually way ahead of the curve. With good reason, a lot of environmentalists and the media are currently focused on conserving energy. But water shortages may become the new global warming (by which I mean the next hot environmental topic). Though there's quite a bit of water on the planet, only about 1 percent of it is usable for humans. This isn't a problem just for people living in the middle of the desert. In the United States, where water use has tripled in the past fifty years, thirty-six states are predicting water shortages by 2013.

So conserving water now is being ahead of the next big thing. And that, of course, is very chic.

POP LITTLE PURCHASES IN YOUR PURSE

When you buy a lipstick from a beauty boutique, or spot a pretty pair of vintage earrings, or pick up a small candle to give as a hostess gift, decline the glossy, logo-bedecked bag the shop probably wants to give you. Note: I'll say more about makeup (page 102), jewelry (page 133), candles (page 50), and shopping bags (page 118) later. But let's not go crazy right now—we're still taking baby steps. To toss any of the aforementioned items in your purse or work tote is *easy*. You just need to get into the habit of doing it.

And this is a habit worth keeping, because most of those little glossy shopping bags are a mixture of paper bags and plastic laminate. Neither paper nor plastic bags are especially good for the environment (learn why on page 118), but the laminated combination is a hybrid of organic material (paper) and technical material (plastic) that can't be easily—or safely— recycled. So it will likely end up as waste.

Tip: If you ever forget to decline the cute shopping bag, don't just throw it away. It's cute, remember? You could reuse it as a gift bag instead of buying a new one.

TAKE (EVEN SLIGHTLY!) SHORTER SHOWERS

Showers account for around 30 percent of the hot water used in most households, and the showers you and yours take can produce many, many thousands of pounds of CO_2 emissions each year. The amount varies depending on how long and hot your showers are, as well as where you live and whether your area uses coal or natural gas to produce the energy that heats your water. If I were to take one ten-minute shower per day at my apartment in Boston, I would produce about 2,000 pounds of CO_2 annually. Cutting that daily shower to eight minutes would save 400 pounds.

(Note: Taking lukewarm or cool showers is another way to cut CO_2 emissions—but I'm a hot shower addict. I tried to give up the heat, but it just wasn't going to happen.)

If you *really* want to shorten your shower, you need a concrete plan. Start by learning how long you spend in there on a typical day. Estimates don't work. Bring your watch or a clock into the bathroom, but don't take it into the shower. Look at it before you get in, do your normal thing, and look at it again when you get out. Do this for a few days to get a realistic estimate of your standard shower length. I was somewhat horrified to learn mine was longer than ten minutes. More like fifteen-plus minutes. Oops.

I decided to make a drastic reduction to six-minute showers. (It's okay if you aren't quite so extreme—every minute counts.) That's more than enough time if you're strategic: Wash and condition your hair right away and let your conditioner soak in while you're soaping and exfoliating, et cetera, then rinse and get out. I now wear my running watch in the shower, and beating my time limit has become a game. Sometimes I'm out in five minutes. Once I got out in four, but that's because I knew I had a glass of wine waiting for me. (No, this was not first thing in the morning!)

Beauty bonus: Taking shorter showers is great for your skin. Hot water is drying, and I've noticed less flaky skin since I put the kibosh on whiling away a quarter of an hour in the shower. There's another benefit, too: Spending less time in the shower means you can spend more time choosing exactly the right outfit and accessories and still get wherever you're going without stressing about running late.

REDUCE YOUR DRY TIME

Spend fewer minutes with your hair dryer each day. If you're one of those people who can eschew it altogether and still look gorgeous, that's great. Go for it. (Just know that there are a lot of women out there who strongly dislike you.) For me, giving up the hair dryer entirely is not an option. Seriously: Not. Going. To. Happen. Why? I don't want my hair to look like crap. Sure, if I'm in the wilderness for a few days I can shove it wet into a ponytail and not worry too much. But for the most part, I like having good hair days. I'd venture to say I'm a better person on good hair days. However, I don't need to use the hair dryer nearly as much as I did to have those good hair days.

Using my 1875-watt hair dryer for twelve minutes a day equals more than 500 pounds of CO_2 emissions annually. If I cut the time in half, I cut the emissions in half, too. When I let my hair air dry for fifteen to twenty minutes before I start blowing, I can easily get it straight and shiny in six minutes. (It helps if I comb it out right after I get out of the shower.) Some days I can do it faster. Time your normal drying session one day, then try it the next day after some air drying and see how the hair looks.

Tip: If you don't have time to wait, at the very least squeeze out as much water as you can, then squeeze a towel around your hair (don't rub—that just adds frizz), and give it several seconds to soak up even more water before you turn on the hair dryer.

Beauty bonus: Not blasting your hair with heat when it's sopping wet is healthier for your lovely locks—it will probably result in less dryness and frizziness and fewer split ends.

By the way, when you're done with the hair dryer, unplug it. Plugged in, your hair dryer draws (i.e., wastes) some energy even when it's not in use. Which brings me to the next little green thing . . .

UNPLUG UNSIGHTLY CHARGERS

As soon as your cell phone is charged, unplug the charger. When plugged in, a charger draws energy even if it's not attached to the cell phone it's meant to charge—about 5 watts per hour. That's 40 kilowatt hours per year, which throws almost 100 pounds of CO_2 into the environment. Since you're right there unplugging your phone anyway, it will take only another second to unplug the charger, too. It took me about a week to get fully into the habit of doing this, but now it's automatic.

And the unplugging habit can go beyond cell phone chargers. Unplug chargers for your iPod, laptop, PDA, electric toothbrush, digital camera, power drill, and any, um, personal toys that might need charging up. For each charger you keep unplugged instead of leaving it at the ready, you could end up saving another 100 pounds of CO_2. (For information on other items you might unplug for even more CO_2 savings, see page 162.)

Style suggestion: It takes a few extra seconds, but when you're unplugging the charger I suggest putting it out of sight, too. A black plastic thing with a cord dangling from it doesn't enhance anyone's décor. Reserve a drawer, or keep a basket or bin handy for storing chargers—which keeps things tidy *and* means you always know where to look for them. So when you're running late, hunting for your charger won't add to your stress level. (And we all know that stress doesn't make anyone more chic. Think about how calm, cool, and collected Jackie and Audrey always looked. Ah.)

Tip: Be sure to recycle or donate old cell phones. We use cell phones for an average of eighteen months, and if we trash them they may leach arsenic, antimony, lead, and other toxic heavy metals. If incinerated, they release dioxins. Many cell phone stores accept used cell phones to be recycled, or you could donate yours to a nonprofit organization such as Phones 4 Charity (phones4charity.org).

GO COLD

Do all your laundry in cold water. I laughed when I first read about the ecobenefits of doing this—which I'll get to in a second—because my clothes, especially my workout clothes, can get pretty rank. You don't want to be trapped in a small space with my sweaty running attire after a 5-miler. Trust me. But because it's my job to try everything at least once, and because about 90 percent (yup, 90 percent) of the energy consumed by washers—which is about 250 kWh per year, emitting 400 or so pounds of CO_2—is used for heating the water, I gave it a go. I tossed in a pungent selection of yoga gear, running clothes, and grungy jeans I'd worn at least six . . . eight . . . okay, twelve times. Yeah, they were saggy at that point.

The verdict? The cold water worked just fine. My workout gear smelled just as sweet as when I wash it in warm or hot water, and the jeans were totally degrunged and desagged. I became an instant cold water convert.

Style bonus: Washing in cold water means your clothes won't fade as fast. Which is a good thing unless you *want* them to fade, in which case I'd suggest drying them in the sun.

Tip: Worried the cold water won't take care of your toughest stains? (Do I sound like a detergent commercial right now?) Here's the thing—if it's a bad stain, it won't come out in hot water either, and in fact the hot water might cause the stain to set. So don't use that as an excuse. The key is pretreating. Concentrate on the spot in question and rub in a small amount of detergent (ecofriendly detergent—more on that on page 35) before you toss it in the wash. It takes a few extra seconds, but saving your favorite tee or skirt from a stained life is worth the effort.

ADJUST YOUR THERMOSTAT 🐚

Turn your heat down 1 degree in the winter, and set your air conditioner 1 degree higher in the summer. That's a change you probably won't notice—you might want to go for 2 degrees. But even 1 degree makes a difference. If you have electric heat, turning it down 1 degree can save up to 240 pounds of CO_2 annually. For gas heat, the savings is even bigger: up to 320 pounds. Come summer, each degree you raise the temperature saves about 120 pounds of CO_2 per year.

Tip: If you're cutting back on the number of window AC units in your house this year, and you're deciding between one you've had for years and a newer model, go with the new one. Old air conditioners are much less energy efficient, and depending on how old they are, they may use chlorofluorocarbons (CFCs) as a cooling agent. CFCs are known to damage the ozone layer. Newer air conditioners feature hydrochlorofluorocarbons instead, which are 95 percent less damaging to the ozone layer. (Still, they aren't great for ozone—yet another reason to turn down your AC.) Look for Energy Star–rated air conditioning units, which use at least 10 percent less energy than conventional units.

Beauty bonus: Excessive indoor heat and air conditioning contribute to dry air, and therefore to dry skin; turning down the heat and/or AC a little means there's more humidity in the air to hydrate your parched dermis. What's more, an air-conditioned environment may contribute to weight gain—our bodies burn more calories when they have to regulate their own temperature in the heat, and people who experience the normal heat of summertime naturally consume fewer calories.

Tip: Don't automatically turn on the heat or the air conditioning without checking to see whether you need it. If the outside air is at a pleasant temperature, turn off the units completely, and let the air flow through your home. Not only does that save energy, it also helps to clear the air in your home of indoor pollutants—and any musty odors. There's a reason they call it fresh air.

SLOW DOWN! 🍃

Do not—I repeat, do not—go out and replace everything you own, from your makeup to your wardrobe to your furniture, with (theoretically) ecofriendly products. Being ecofriendly means consuming *less*, not more. And if you're buying and buying like crazy, you're definitely on the *more* track. Get in the habit of thinking before you buy. The best time to purchase ecofriendly goods is when you *need* them. That's when you're in a position to make a choice, and express yourself as a consumer. Almost out of toilet paper? Okay, go get that postconsumer recycled roll (see page 39). Mattress sagging painfully? Test the chemical-free, organic options (page 54). Can't live without some sexy jeans? Shop till you drop for vintage or organic. You get the point.

Beware of greenwashing: Take care to avoid products that claim to be green just for the marketing effect. Think about natural Cheetos and Doritos, huge, gas-guzzling hybrid SUVs, clothes boasting that they're green just because they're made from "natural" cotton (which is actually nasty for the environment when grown conventionally), beauty products claiming to be "natural" when they actually contain a long list of unhealthy chemicals, and anything that purports to be "recycled" without telling you what components are actually recycled and what they are recycled from. Green is trendy, and companies out there are taking advantage by trying to greenwash consumers. Don't believe the hype.

I explain all this in the next several chapters, and when you're done reading, you'll be a savvy consumer—and you can be confident that everything you *do* buy is green chic.

A few chic things that have always been green

- Going barefoot on the beach in a linen dress
- Beauty sleep
- Owning your personal style instead of following every trend
- Eating lobster on the coast of Maine
- Your great-grandmother's wedding band
- A perfectly tailored, impeccably made wool coat
- Linen napkins
- Skinny-dipping
- A vintage Chanel jacket
- Giving thoughtful gifts you know the recipient will *love*

- An exquisite antique table
- A luxurious, high-quality cashmere sweater
- Sharing oysters on Tomales Bay with a bottle of Grgich Hills Sauvignon Blanc
- Beautiful family heirlooms
- Keeping your clothes and furniture in perfect condition
- A table set with vintage white china and lit by beeswax candles
- Moonlight (nothing's more naturally flattering)
- Smiling

Chapter Three

HOME, GREEN HOME

Pardonnez-moi while I wax sentimental: Home should be a sanctuary, a place that feels safe and healthy, looks beautiful, and smells wonderful. Seriously. Whether you're in a little city apartment (I'm right there with you) or a pad in the 'burbs (so jealous of your closet space right now), make it a place that you can come to and have an immediate feeling of . . . *Aaaaah. I'm home. Awesome.*

You don't need to hire a decorator or buy all new stuff or take on a new mortgage. Greening your house will go a long way toward making wherever you are an oasis. A green home is the most sanctuary-like home around—by which I mean it's beautiful and healthy and it smells terrific.

Making your home greener does not require foregoing your personal style. (Then it wouldn't be your personal sanctuary. Duh.) Everyone has different taste in home décor, and there's no need to sacrifice your penchant for, say, midcentury modern or girly antiques or whatever it is you love and get all rough-hewn, handmade furnishings. Personally, I like a beach cottage vibe and lots of clean white and natural tones. And I dislike tchotchkes. A lot.

That's a big part of making your home green: getting to know what you like and don't like instead of following trends—and understanding what really makes you happy so you don't have to keep shopping for it. If you do that, and learn about the environmental and health hazards lurking in way too much home stuff, your space will look and feel great no matter *how* you choose to adorn it. I hope this chapter will help!

P.S. I've divided the chapter into two sections, one about smaller stuff that's fairly easy to change (cleaning products, toilet paper—yes, there are green chic options in these categories) and one about more permanent items (furniture, paint, and other stuff for which it's a good idea to avoid buyer's remorse).

Part I: Smaller stuff

CLEAN GREEN

Use cleaning products that:

- list their ingredients (many conventional cleaners don't)
- contain no chlorine, anything that starts with chlor, or ammonia
- are certified biodegradable and free of synthetic chemicals
- come in recyclable packaging

There are many reasons for all this, which I'll explain in a minute. Before I do, let me say that earth-friendly cleaning products can *really* work. I wouldn't recommend them if they didn't.

Take, for instance, all-purpose spray cleaner. This is my go-to cleaner.

A little bit of background on my attachment to it: I never sit on public toilets. I'm not obsessive-compulsive in many areas, but I am in public bathrooms. There's some serious nastiness going on in there. When I have to pee, I squat and hover. I never touch. The benefits are twofold. Most importantly, I don't get skeeved out thinking about what my skin is touching. The mini quad workout I get is nice, too. (It's kind of like utkatasana—the chair pose—in yoga.) But that's really secondary.

In my own bathroom, I really, really used to like using Fantastik spray cleaner. A lot of it. (This is related to my public bathroom thing—the connection should become clear in a second.) I wasn't always this way. Sure, I cleaned my bathroom as much as the next person. Okay, maybe not that much. Then I started dating a guy who peed on the rim of every toilet he ever used. No, not just on the rim. Once he got comfortable in a place, he seemed to lose all sense of direction and pee would wind up on the rim, the backside of the seat (if he remembered to put it up), and the seat itself. It would sometimes drip down the sides of the toilet. And, in his bathroom—which went uncleaned for long stretches—it would leave quite a residue all over the floor.

That's when I became a Fantastik freak. And even when Pee Guy was gone, the Fantastik stayed. I used it all over the bathroom and in the kitchen, too.

But like so many things we use without thinking much about them, conventional chemical spray cleaners aren't great for the environment—outside and especially inside your home. Conventional cleaners release volatile organic compounds and other toxic chemicals that remain on your home's surfaces and evaporate into the air. These cleaners are the second-biggest contributor—behind pesticides—to the fact that the air inside most homes is two to five times more polluted than the air outside. What's more, this stuff is seeping out of our homes— not that we really want to keep it inside with us—and into the environment. Almost 70 percent of streams sampled in a 2002 study by the U.S. Geological Survey contained chemicals from household cleaning products.

These chemicals are bad for you: About 10 percent of toxic exposures reported to U.S. Poison Control Centers are related to cleaning products directly touching the skin or being ingested. Chlorine bleach (a big component of many cleaners) can burn skin and eyes and can be fatal if it's swallowed. And it releases organochlorines, VOCs that have been shown—even at very low levels—to cause cancer, hormonal changes, reproductive disorders, neurological problems, and immune system disorders. (Organochlorines also react with just about everything in their path to create new toxins, and they travel through the environment very fast.) If every household in the U.S. replaced just one bottle of conventional chemical cleaning spray with a biodegradable, ecofriendly product, that would keep 11 million pounds of VOCs from entering the environment. Ammonia, another cleaning star ingredient, is poisonous if ingested and is a respiratory irritant. If accidentally mixed together, ammonia and chlorine create a toxic gas.

To add insult to injury, much of this stuff comes in nonrecyclable containers. One label I read on a nonrecyclable bottle of all-purpose spray cleaner actually admonishes you to throw the empty bottle away *in the trash.*

When I learned all this, I was ready to switch to a healthier (for the environment and the human body) spray cleaner. And my conventional spray was just about gone. Unfortunately, this all came together for me the same weekend Will had a boys' night out and four of his drunk friends ended up crashing at our apartment. Will, to his credit, is not a pee-on-the-seat kind of guy. Or if he is I don't know about it, because he cleans up after himself. I do love that. His friends, however (at least when they've been drinking), aren't quite so careful. So there was bathroom cleanup to be done, *sans le Fantastique.* Oy.

Books and articles I read about ecofriendly housekeeping gave different recipes for various combinations of white vinegar, lemon juice, and borax—unique ideas for every cleaning conundrum. Um, no. I'm an all-purpose cleaner kind of gal, and not so much into home remedies for cleaning toilets. (I have tried the white vinegar, and while it does a nice job cleaning glass, it doesn't leave my bathroom or kitchen with a particularly appealing fragrance.)

There are a variety of companies that make ecofriendly, sweet-smelling, and effective cleaning products. And that's what I used to clean up the drunk-Saturday-night-pee-on-and-near-the-toilet. The ecofriendly spray cleaner I chose came in a spray bottle, so I could wield it just like my Fantastik. It did a fabulous job cleaning up the pee. I felt so confident in the results that I used the toilet soon thereafter. Yes, I sat on the seat—no squatting or hovering.

My favorite ecofriendly cleaning brand is Method (methodhome.com)—the packaging is really cool and recyclable, everything smells good, and it works. (Note: In the interest of maintaining a commitment to gorgeously minimalist design, Method doesn't list ingredients on their bottles—but they do list ingredients for every product on their website. And it's good stuff.) Method's products are made from materials such as soy, coconut, essential oils, and naturally derived surfactants that absorb dirt instead of chemically degrading it, which is what standard chemical cleaners do. Seventh Generation and Planet also make nice and effective products, and I've recently become a fan of Mrs. Meyer's Clean Day (mrsmeyers.com) products, too. Yes, they're a little more expensive, but not overwhelmingly so. At a grocery store in San Francisco—the most expensive grocery store I've ever shopped in—the ever-popular Fantastik all-purpose spray was $4.29 for 32 ounces, or 13.41¢ per ounce, and Comet bathroom spray was $3.09 for 17 ounces, or 18.2¢ per ounce. By comparison, Method (the chicest) was $5.29 for 28 ounces (18.89¢ per ounce) and Planet was $3.95 for 22 ounces (17.95¢ per ounce).

Keep in mind: The rules at the beginning of this section apply to all cleaning products. For dish soap and detergent, also avoid phosphates, which can damage water systems, and anything derived from petroleum, which is a nonrenewable resource. (For info on petroleum in laundry products, see the sidebar on page 35.)

Shopping strategy: If your grocery store or drugstore doesn't carry any earth-friendly cleaning products, ask them to start, and buy your products online, from nearby green home stores, or the closest Whole Foods. Method is available at Target (target.com), and you can find Mrs. Meyer's everywhere from drugstores to natural food stores to Dean & Deluca in Manhattan.

Tip: Remember that white vinegar mixed with water (about a one-to-one ratio) works in a pinch and is especially good for cleaning glass. If you decide to mix your own cleaner, don't mix anything with chemical-containing commercial cleaners, and always label it, so that you remember what it is and don't try to turn it into salad dressing a few months later.

Dirty laundry

Detergent: Standard laundry detergent is derived from petroleum via an energy-intensive process (almost a pound of greenhouse gases emitted for every little *ounce* of detergent produced) and contains hormone-disrupting phthalates. If possible, choose petroleum- and phthalate-free detergent. Method and Mrs. Meyer's make healthy, biodegradable detergents that I really like. And if you must have your Tide, buy concentrated detergents in the largest sized bottle you can find to cut down on packaging.

Bleach: Chlorine bleach is caustic and can be fatal if swallowed. It can also react with other chemicals to produce dioxins. Try hydrogen peroxide in lieu of basic bleach to get your whites whiter and all that.

Fabric softeners: In liquid form, they often contain neurotoxins (including toluene, which you can read more about on page 95) and respiratory irritants, and some are made from animal by-products. And they build up on clothes over time and make them look shabby. Fabric-softening dryer sheets may also contain animal by-products, as well as synthetic fragrances (featuring not-so-fabulous formaldehyde, and more phthalates). Look for biodegradable, plant-derived products.

Tip: Greenhome.com is a good source for ecofriendly home supplies, including paper products, cleaners, and detergents, as well as bigger ticket home goods, from vacuum cleaners to armoires.

BE PICKY ABOUT PAPER PRODUCTS 🖋

Whenever possible, opt for reusable alternatives to household paper products (think napkins and paper towels). And when that's not a viable option (hello, toilet paper), choose 100 percent recycled products. Think your paper use doesn't make much difference? The tissue you use to blow your nose might not weigh much, but it adds up: Americans go through 741 pounds of paper each per year. That's the equivalent of chopping down about four and a half trees per person every year. Yes, trees are a renewable resource—but only truly so if they are forested responsibly. Many large paper companies clear-cut forests and damage ecosystems with their logging practices.

And though deforestation is a concern, it's not the only one. Producing virgin paper is an extremely energy-intensive process, and the virgin-paper-producing industry is the third-biggest industrial contributor to global warming. Paper that's not recycled winds up in landfills—about 40 percent of all trash in U.S. landfills consists of paper products. Typical household paper products are bleached with chlorine or a chlorine derivative, a process that releases dioxins into the environment.

So how can you cut your use of virgin paper products? Let's break it down.

Paper towels: If every U.S. household replaced one roll of standard paper towels with a reusable towel or 100 percent recycled paper towels, that would save more than half a million trees. To clean up spills and wipe counters, try sponges—*not* the antibacterial kind, because you don't need to bring more chemicals into your life—instead of paper towels, and to keep them from getting nasty and smelling bad, rinse and squeeze them out after using and leave them standing on their side so they dry quickly. (That's Will's trick, and it works well. He's very proud of that one and gets a little annoyed with me when I forget to do it—but hey, everyone has *one* flaw, right?) And throw them in your dishwasher every time you run it to zap germs. Real towels (preferably made from organic cotton or hemp) work, too, and so do rags cut from old T-shirts (just toss 'em in with your laundry). If you're hooked on the convenience of disposable paper towels, look for brands that are 100 percent recycled (with at least 80

percent postconsumer waste content) and chlorine-free, such as
Seventh Generation (seventhgen.com) and Planet (planet.com).

Napkins: I'm trying to think of a time when using paper
napkins might be chic. Can't come up with one. (Having a messy
backyard barbecue? Cloth napkins will make it nicer—get brightly
colored ones so the stains won't show.) Cloth napkins are more
elegant every time. And more ecofriendly—if every American
household gave up just one package of 250 paper napkins in
exchange for reusable napkins or 100 percent recycled napkins,
that would save a million trees. Choose reusable napkins in
organic cotton, linen, or hemp—and if you find *some* reason to
purchase paper napkins, look for at least 80 percent postconsumer
waste and chlorine-free, such as Seventh Generation and the 365
Everyday Value napkins from Whole Foods.

Tissues: I love it when people have aha! green moments and
share them with me. My sister, Jen, called me one day to tell me
that she had a cold and that she had gone through a big box of
tissues and was about to dive into another one when she realized
how wasteful it was. So she was excited to look into other
options. She found a set of reusable organic cotton hankies,
and—ever the thoughtful and practical gift-giver—got some for
me too, for Christmas. Hankettes (hankettes.com) makes them,
along with organic cotton dish towels, tea towels, and cleaning
cloths. (My sis also had a tree planted for me. Aw.) Anyway, she
was right. Eliminating one box of virgin tissues per household
would save more than 150,000 trees. The organic hankies are
super—and so soft. And you just wash them after a use or two.

Alternatively, go for 100 percent recycled tissues (at least 80 percent postconsumer) that are chlorine-free.

TP: Toilet paper use got a lot of attention in 2007 when Sheryl Crow suggested a ban on toilet paper. (She later said she was joking, but I think she caved.) Anyway, thinking about reducing toilet paper consumption is very chic. And green: If every household in the United States replaced a five-hundred-sheet roll of virgin toilet paper with 100 percent recycled toilet paper, we'd save more than four hundred thousand trees. Now, I've read suggestions about reusing your bathroom wiping apparatuses (or is it apparati?). I'm not going to repeat them here. That's beyond yucky. Buy recycled toilet paper, and as with paper towels, look for brands that are 100 percent recycled, at least 80 percent postconsumer waste content, and chlorine-free. Again, Seventh Generation products are a good bet. Want to take it a step further? Heed Ms. Crow's wise words and try to spare a square or two each time—you generally don't need wads of the stuff to get the job done.

Feeling flush

Talk of toilets and the environment often brings up the edict "If it's yellow let it mellow; if it's brown, flush it down." Lovely, yes? The idea is that regular toilets use anywhere from 3.5 to 5 gallons (or more) of water per flush, so flushing less means using less water. (Toilets can account for more than 40 percent of a household's water usage, so this is worth considering.)

I get it, conceptually, but I have decided that I am not going to leave my pee in the toilet. I tried it for a few days, then I accidentally "let it mellow" for more than a week while I was traveling. My bathroom did not smell very nice when I returned. My eyes water a little bit now when I think about it. I know that's an extreme case, but I also don't want a guest to come over and find the yellow—and used (recycled, of course) toilet paper—in the bowl. Call me old-fashioned, but I think a gracious hostess greets her guests with a clean loo.

Another option is to use less water with each flush. If you're installing a new toilet for some reason, go for a water-conserving model, which uses around 1.5 gallons per flush. If, like me, you're stuck in a rental apartment with old plumbing, find an old disposable water bottle or two (you know, from before you stopped drinking out of those) or a milk jug or some other bottle, weight it with a handful of pebbles and fill it with water, and stick it in your toilet tank, making sure not to interfere with any of the gizmos in there. This displaces water in the tank, meaning less will go down the drain with each flush. The more water you displace, the less you flush. It's that simple.

Note to water displacers: There are inexpensive water displacing devices you can buy, but why spend money on something as unglamorous as a toilet water displacer? And you may have heard that a brick in the toilet is a good way to displace water, but actually bricks can break down over time and kink up that magical flushing mechanism. So far the milk jugs are working just fine for me—and the flushing is as effective as ever.

Note to apartment renters: If your toilet (or faucet) is leaking, call your landlord and get it fixed. That's one benefit of not owning—someone else can do the dirty work.Leaks are responsible for up to 14 percent of home water usage; if it's leaking a drop of water per second, that's 2,700 gallons a year.

Plastics primer

Plastic is everywhere. And it sure seems convenient. But it isn't very chic. I've never seen a plastic vase or a plastic-covered sofa that was especially stylish. It isn't green, either. Manufacturing plastic requires huge amounts of natural resources and energy. The process also releases significant toxic chemicals into the environment—it's responsible for the release of almost 15 percent of the most dangerous industrial toxins (such as styrene, benzene, and dioxins) into the air. Plastic production also emits sulfur oxides, nitrous oxides, methanol, ethylene oxide, and VOCs. Most plastic is derived from petroleum (I've said it before, and I'll say it again: a nonrenewable resource), which is cranked up to almost 800 degrees (remember how turning the heat in your home down 1 degree saves 240 pounds of CO_2 per year?) before it's broken down into the polymers that are combined with other chemicals and shaped into various types of plastic. Plastic can never completely biodegrade.

But at least it can be recycled, right? Well, maybe. Not all plastics are created equal, not all plastics can be easily and safely recycled, and different types of plastic can't be recycled together. **And just because you see the triangular arrows with a number inside on the bottom of a plastic container doesn't mean it can be recycled.** It's the number inside that matters. There are seven major varieties of plastics that consumers see, and part of living green is getting to know the numbers. I know, I know, this sounds like a pain in the ass—but trust me, it's not that bad. Hang with me for a sec. The numbers are easy to remember: one through seven.

If you take nothing else away from this section, remember that numbers three, six, and seven are the ones to avoid if at all possible, because they can't be recycled easily and because they leach chemicals over the course of their (very long) lifetimes. Here's a quick look at all the numbers:

#1: Polyethylene terephthalate (PET or PETE) makes most disposable water bottles and soda bottles. It is not meant for reuse. This plastic is fairly easy to recycle, and most recycling facilities accept it.

#2: High density polyethylene (HDPE) makes many toys, milk bottles, detergent bottles, and shampoo bottles. Like PET, HDPE is fairly easy to recycle and is accepted at most facilities.

#3: Polyvinyl chloride (vinyl or PVC) makes pipe, shower curtains, some flip-flops, some food wrap, toys, wallpaper, many yoga mats, and much more. **This is the worst of all the common consumer plastics**. I bolded that for a reason. If you don't want to store data for numbers six and seven in your brain, at the very least remember this one—and skip it. Producing PVC is incredibly energy-intensive, and its manufacture requires massive amounts of chlorine and releases dioxin, a toxic, carcinogenic, hormone-disrupting, immune-system-damaging chemical. About seven billion pounds of PVC are discarded annually in the United States and most recycling facilities won't accept it, because recycling it is highly labor-intensive and potentially hazardous. If PVC is mixed in with other plastics at a recycling facility, it can contaminate the whole batch. If it goes to a landfill instead, it leaches lead and phthalates into soil and groundwater. If it gets incinerated, that's even worse—because PVC contains chlorine, burning it releases more dioxins into the environment.

#4: Low density polyethylene (LDPE) makes plastic wrap and grocery bags. It's fairly easy and effective to recycle, but many recycling facilities aren't set up to recycle it.

#5: Polypropylene (PP) makes yogurt tubs and diapers. Like LDPE, polypropylene can be safely and effectively recycled, but it's not widely accepted at recycling facilities.

#6: Polystyrene (PS) is usually referred to by the trademarked name Styrofoam, and it shows up in lots of coffee cups and takeout containers. It may leach styrene, a possible carcinogen and hormone disruptor, into food and hot beverages. And it's not easy to recycle.

#7: Other could be a variety of things, but it's usually polycarbonate, and it's the plastic of most baby bottles, 5-gallon water jugs, and some hikers' water bottles. It may leach the chemical bisphenol-A (BPA), an endocrine disruptor. It is recyclable, but not universally accepted.

You know what? All this is kind of a pain in the ass. Another good rule of thumb is to pass over plastic—period—whenever you can. If you've got a choice between plastic and no plastic at all, you know what to do.

FILL THE FRIDGE 🐚

Refrigerators are the energy-suckingest appliance in most homes. If yours isn't Energy Star–rated, it probably accounts for about 14 percent of your electricity use, which means it kicks off almost 1.5 tons of greenhouse gases per year. Energy Star–rated fridges use anywhere from 20 to 50 percent less energy.

No matter what kind of fridge you've got, make it more efficient by keeping it full—a full fridge loses less cold air when the door is opened. I don't like having a refrigerator full of processed foods (if they're there, I might eat them), and if you overdo it on the fresh produce it'll go bad. My friend Casey came up with a brilliant—and very chic—solution: Fill it with white wine. Okay, not *just* with white wine. Rosé and Champagne, too. (Yes, yes, and some milk and juice and stuff.) But why not pick up a whole case of your favorite to-be-chilled wine—

preferably organic or biodynamic—and keep it in the fridge? That way you'll always have some on hand if you're invited to a last-minute dinner party, guests show up unannounced, or you just need some late one night. If you do that, and vacuum the coils once or twice a year, and don't gape at the contents with the door open, you could save up to 20 percent of the energy your fridge is using.

More fridge advice, in case you want it: Keep the temp between 38 and 40 degrees—that's plenty cool to keep food safe, and if you're keeping it between 28 and 32 you're using about 25 percent more energy.

Tip: Fill the dishwasher, too.

Only run the dishwasher when it's full. You'll cut down on water and energy use—if you run the dishwasher one time less per week, you'll keep about one hundred pounds of CO_2 out of the environment.

Curtains on PVC shower curtains

If you're buying a new shower curtain, get one that's PVC-free. (Are you picking up on the whole "no PVC" theme I've got going?) Many shower curtains are made of vinyl. At this point you know the downsides of vinyl. Shower curtains are another large PVC home item—and they are generally located in small rooms where the air gets steamy and you're forced to be in very close proximity to all those plasticizers.

Then, of course, there are the aesthetic problems. PVC shower curtains, in my opinion, look cheap and tacky. And they smell funny. (Those fumes are not good for you.)

Healthier, ecofriendly shower curtain alternatives include organic cotton (look for a tight weave so that it resists water better, and wash and air dry it if it gets moldy), linen (Gaiam (gaiam.com) carries a cool flax-colored one; linen is more mildew-resistant than cotton), or hemp. Apparently less attractive from an eco standpoint, but still far, far, far superior to (and safer than) PVC is nylon pack cloth. Nylon is a petroleum-based fabric that has an energy-intensive production process—but then again, most natural textiles have energy-intensive production processes, too. And a nylon pack cloth curtain is washable and will last pretty much 4-eva, meaning you won't have to go out and buy yet another energy-intensive product. You can get a cool pack cloth curtain for about fifty bucks (linen and hemp curtains might run a smidge higher)—more than a PVC curtain, sure, but having to replace a ratty PVC curtain every couple of years won't save dough in the long run. Check out Satara Home & Baby Store (satara-inc.com) for a great selection of shower curtains, including pack cloth options.

If you have a PVC shower curtain, don't panic. Oh, and do not set it on fire. ('Cause I know you were about to.) Burning vinyl releases dioxons—yes, that's like the tenth time I've said that—which are much, much, much worse for you than the chemicals that shower curtains off-gas into the air in their non-inflamed state. Keep your bathroom as well ventilated as possible—window(s) opened, vent fan on while you're in there, all that jazz. And hey, why not take shorter showers? (I explain why and how on page 20.)

CUT CLUTTER ✍

First and foremost, getting rid of clutter is a simple (though not exactly easy) way to make your home more fabulous without buying a thing. The times when I dislike my apartment the most are when there's junk everywhere. Magazines piled on the floor. Unpaid bills on my desk. Dirty clothes overflowing from my laundry bags. Clean clothes not put away. CDs and CD cases strewn about. Ok, I'm going to stop this list now, because I sound like a major slob. The point is, when all that crud is everywhere, my apartment isn't very welcoming. And sometimes that makes me think I need all new stuff. Which I don't. What I need to do is to get rid of the mess.

There are ecobenefits to doing so, too—having less clutter means you won't be tempted to come home one day and throw away *everything* without recycling. Also, and this might sound gross but it's true, without clutter it's easier to spot little pests like ants immediately, if and when they show up. They've got nowhere to hide. So the problem doesn't get out of control, and you won't have to resort to pesticides. And your place will look really nice *sans* crap.

Here are tips for dealing with common clutter causers.

Magazines: Only keep subscriptions to magazines you actually read regularly and would miss if they weren't around. Aside from the fact that only about 5 percent of magazines use *any* recycled content in their paper, and that most magazine paper is bleached with chlorine (which, as I've said, releases carcinogenic dioxins), magazines pile up and make your house look messy. If they're highbrow titles, you'll feel guilty for neglecting them. Eliminate the stress and the stacks by canceling unnecessary subscriptions. Give the ones you do get to friends after you read them.

Bills: Pay all your bills online and stop the paper versions from coming to your house. That will save time and keep your desk much neater. Did you ever notice all that excess stuff that comes with a bill? It might not add up to hundreds of pounds of paper per year in your house, but every little bit saved helps.

Junk mail: The production and disposal of a year's worth of junk mail slays more than one hundred million trees, wastes 28 billion gallons of water, and pumps out as much CO_2 as 2.8 million cars. Sign up for a service such as 41 Pounds (41pounds.org), and you'll be off most lists for five years (for the so-worth-it fee of $41). And both your mailbox and your desk will be cleared of more clutter.

CDs: Stop buying them and download music onto a tiny little iPod (apple.com) instead. CDs and their cases are made from an energy-intensive mix (mix—get it? Like a music mix?) of such materials as polycarbonate, paper, aluminum, and—uh oh— PVC. Plus they leave a heap o' junk when you're searching for the Springsteen disc you actually put away in the Killers case. iPods (I know they aren't the only MP3 players out there, but I think they rock—get it? Rock? Like rock music?) aren't perfect, but Apple is working to get greener, and they will take back and recycle parts of worn-out pods.

Clothes: Keep up with the laundry and put clean clothes away. (I just sounded like my mother.) The reason is twofold: First, it helps straighten up the joint. Second, it enables you to select from your entire wardrobe in the morning, thereby leading to a more fulfilling wardrobe experience. (For more on the ecobenefits of liking your clothes, turn to the fashion chapter on page 115).

They're not really clutter . . .

Every surface of your home needn't be totally barren. I'd still advise immediate removal of any and all tchotchkes, but plants and candles can be delightful, chic, and very green—not just colorly speaking.

Plants: Not only are plants kinda pretty (I don't mean tacky spider plants but *nice* ones, hopefully organic ones), but they help eliminate toxins such as formaldehyde, toluene, xylene, trichloroethylene, and benzene from your interior. Here are five chic ones—hello, orchids—to add. If possible, go for long-lasting plants instead of cut flowers that you'll have to toss in a few days.

- Gerber daisies (reduce formaldehyde levels)
- Chrysanthemums (reduce benzene and trichloroethylene levels)
- Orchids (reduce xylene and toluene levels)
- English ivy (reduces benzene levels)
- Bamboo (reduces formaldehyde levels)

Candles: Shut off the lights and fire up some soy or beeswax candles (not petroleum-based paraffin ones). Soy candles might sound hippie, but you can find drop-dead elegant versions—and they last longer and smoke less than standard paraffin candles. Make sure the wicks are lead-free, so your new flame doesn't emit toxic fumes, and steer clear of artificially, chemically-scented candles, which may contain phthalates. The pure soy candles from Kobo (kobocandles.com) smell and look fantastic, and Aveda (aveda.com) has a stunning, simple white soy candle that comes in a 95 percent recycled glass holder.

CREATE A CUTE RECYCLING SETUP

The implicit suggestion here is that you should recycle. You've heard that before, although you may not have heard why. So I'll explain why—and how to do it in a way that's easy and looks good.

Even though not every plastic, paper, and aluminum item you send to your friendly neighborhood recycler will actually *be* recycled, it's still worth trying. The U.S. recycles more than 2.3 million tons of glass bottles, fifty-four billion aluminum cans, and countless billions of plastic and paper pieces.

A recycled aluminum can requires only 5 percent of the energy needed to produce a brand-new one. Recycling glass instead of making new glass saves 50 percent of production energy. A ton of recycled paper means 60 percent less energy consumed, seventeen trees saved, and 7,000 gallons of water conserved. If everyone recycled her Sunday paper, we'd save a million trees a week. Let's keep it up.

The only way you're going to recycle habitually is if you make it really easy to do. This doesn't mean you need to set up bulky, ugly plastic recycling bins in the middle of your house. Please. That doesn't go with green chic décor. But you could set up several sassy containers like baskets, canvas totes (it's tough to beat an L.L. Bean Boat & Tote bag), or cool bins made from repurposed wood (the chalkboard bins from VivaTerra (vivaterra.com) are made from reclaimed barn wood), clearly labeled with the type of recycling you can toss in. Keep separate bins for plastic, glass, metal, and paper (and, depending on your local recycling rules, possibly further separate the different types of plastic—see page 42). Doing this helps make the recycling process more efficient and reduces contamination. Different materials can't be recycled together, and adding just a bit of something foreign to the stew can ruin a big batch of recycling.

Get in the habit of breaking down your recyclables into their component parts, too: Remove caps and labels from bottles, take the plastic bags out of cereal boxes, that kind of thing. Yeah, it's hassle-ish—but soon it will become second nature. And you can admire your array of snazzy recycling receptacles while you work.

Part II: Bigger stuff

SLEEP IN ORGANIC SHEETS

Unless they're organic, the cotton sheets on your bed were probably sprayed with about 1.25 pounds of pesticides. Conventionally grown cotton uses 25 percent of the world's insecticides and 10 percent of all pesticides. Those not-so-delightful concoctions are carcinogens, and they seep into groundwater and contaminate the habitats of fish and other wildlife. Regular cotton sheets are also usually treated with formaldehyde (a carcinogen, throat irritant, and headache inducer, among other things) and either colored with dyes that may contain heavy metals and carcinogens (about half of those dyes seep out of factories and into soil and groundwater) or bleached with chlorine, a process that releases vile, carcinogenic dioxins. No wonder my mom always told me to wash new sheets before sleeping in them.

Are cotton-polyester blends better? Don't even get me started on those. Ew. (I'm really picky about sheets.) Okay, the quick scoop on cotton-poly sheets is that, in addition to being scratchier than all-cotton sheets, they tend to pill more quickly and don't last as long. Meaning you have to go out and buy another set (not green). Plus polyester is derived from petroleum, and its production requires serious CO_2-emitting energy. So please: Put down the poly blends.

Now, if going organic meant giving up fabulous sheets, I'd have to think twice about it. As I mentioned before, I am particular about sheets. Perhaps more particular about sheets than anything else in my house, which is why I put this at the top of the list. (We're all material girls about some things— whatever you're picky about is a great place to start going green.) Admittedly, there are other things you could do in your home that would have a bigger impact on your environmental footprint. But dude, you get so intimate with your sheets. There's skin-on-sheet contact for many hours per night. You're *sleeping* with them—and we should all be very choosy about who and what we sleep with. No?

When it's time to buy sheets, look for sets made from organic cotton (or linen, or pesticide-free bamboo) that are free of harsh chemical dyes and aren't bleached with chlorine. Anna Sova (annasova.com) makes gorgeous organic sheets that start around $130 for a complete set, and the organic sheets from Coyuchi (coyuchiorganic.com) start around $50 (flat and fitted sold separately). I'm currently obsessed with the supersoft and superchic sheets from Loop (looporganic.com). They aren't the cheapest organic option (approximately $200 for a complete sheet set), but they will be around for a long time. Unlike an unworthy one-night stand.

Tip: Keep an extra organic cotton or organic wool blanket around so you can get cozy on winter nights without turning up the heat.

Throw in the towel

Remember all those pesticides and chemical finishers in conventional cotton sheets? Yeah, they're in conventional cotton towels, too. Which you're rubbing all over your naked body when you get out of the shower. Many towels are also treated with triclosan, a chemical antibacterial agent that may react to create chloroform. Manufacturing triclosan releases dioxins, and the use of chemical antibacterials such as triclosan promotes the development of treatment-resistant bacteria. Dry off with an untreated organic cotton towel, or a pesticide-free bamboo towel, which has natural antibacterial properties. Pottery Barn (potterybarn.com) and West Elm (westelm.com) offer organic cotton towels, as well as sheets and a few other bed and bath goodies.

KNOW YOUR MATTRESS MATTERS 🛏

Continuing with the theme of being careful about what and whom you allow in your boudoir . . . when it's time for a new mattress, choose a chemical-free wool one. Preferably one filled with natural latex instead of polyurethane foam, and made from sustainably harvested, untreated wood instead of particleboard or plywood that contains formaldehyde. Yeah, that's a lot to think about—but there's a lot that goes into a mattress.

Chemical-free is the first thing to look for. The U.S. Consumer Product Safety Commission requires that mattresses and box springs meet minimum standards of fire resistance— and so most mattresses are treated with fire-retardant chemicals such as polybrominated diphenyl ethers (PBDEs). This is some bad schizz—PBDEs accumulate in humans exposed to products that contain them, and may promote the growth of breast cancer cells in women and interfere with brain development in children, among other things. (Washington and California have passed bans on certain forms of PBDEs and are phasing them out over the course of several years.) Chemical-free wool is a natural fire retardant and a good alternative. As for the filling in a mattress, polyurethane foam is usually present. It's often treated with PBDEs, too, and off-gases toxic VOCs like toluene. Look for mattresses filled with natural latex or a spring system surrounded by organic cotton batting. North Star Beds (northstarbed.com) are handmade by the Amish (really), and you can customize the firmness of each side so you and your bed-mate can retreat and sleep well. They're pricey, starting around $1100, but they are extremely well-made. EcoBedroom (ecobedroom.com) carries a variety of chemical-free mattresses, starting in the $800 range and going up—in some cases *way* up—from there. All products from IKEA (ikea.com) aren't totally organic, but they are PBDE-free, including mattresses, which start at prices under $200.

Tip: If investing in a new mattress isn't happening anytime soon, consider covering your current one with a wool or organic mattress pad or barrier cloth to keep the chemicals where they belong (i.e., away from you). Furnature (furnature.com) makes them, and they start around $150. The organic barrier cloths from Heart of Vermont (heartofvermont.com) are comparably priced.

TO SHOP OR NOT TO (FURNITURE) SHOP

Unless you're going uber-minimalist, furniture is the most prominent feature (other than walls and ceilings and stuff) in your house. From a green living perspective, it's a huge topic. There are the raw materials (where they come from, how they're obtained), the manufacturing process, the glues and finishes, the textiles, the fillings, the waste, the shipping . . . I know. Overwhelming.

So let's start with an easy idea: **Don't go out and get new furniture unless you really need it.** The idea of greening your home does not, not, *not* require you to go out and replace everything you've got with new ecofriendly stuff. (New stuff takes energy to produce and the process of manufacturing emits toxic chemicals—and you'd have to get rid of your old stuff, which means it might end up in a landfill, taking up space and leaching chemicals, or being incinerated and releasing even worse chemicals. Again, overwhelming.)

Okay, but say you really do need something. Here are a few ideas to keep in mind.

Think vintage: There's a reason hordes of shoppers flock to high-end antique shops and fairs on weekends—you can find furniture that's gorgeous with a capital G, carefully made with a capital C, and ecofriendly with a capital E (because it requires no energy now to produce something that was made a long time ago, and because furniture made in the days of yore was made better than furniture made in the days of swell, after yore, so it will last longer and you won't need to replace it). Though I tend to find antiquing boring with a capital B, I recently picked up a fabu little writing desk from the late 1800s. I didn't spend days trolling for it—I asked my friend who actually *likes* antique shops to keep an eye out for me 'cause I was in desk-need, and she told me exactly where to go. It cost about $150 and was in practically perfect condition— my research suggests there was no way I was getting anything that good new for less than $600. Just don't buy anything with peeling lead paint.

Style bonus: Buying vintage furniture means your living room won't look like everyone else's living room. Before I saw the green light (had to get that pun in this book somewhere) I ordered a couch from a certain chain furniture store. The one everybody orders from. The couch everybody has. Something with a *wee* bit of uniqueness might have been more fun. Ah, well. It's white, and I like it, and I'm not going to buy a new one right now.

Refurbish: Sprucing up an existing piece uses 85 to 95 percent less energy than producing a new one. So have that table refinished (with low-VOC products) or that sofa reupholstered (with sustainable or vintage fabric).

Look for furniture made from repurposed and recycled materials: Check out a Brooklyn-based company called Scrapile (scrapile.com) that uses wood scraps from a piano factory to make furniture and home accessories. Cool, right?

If you wood: When buying new wood furniture, make sure the wood is certified by the Forest Stewardship Council (FSC). The United States is the world's biggest consumer of wood (surprisingly enough—kidding), so our consumption habits make a difference. And there's a difference to be made: Only about 20 percent of forests around the world remain undamaged enough to provide a long-term habitat for native plants and animals. Deforestation is continuing at a mad fast pace, almost 32 million acres annually. That's not good for global warming, because though trees can't solve the problem, they do help cool the planet, sucking a lot of the CO_2 we're pumping out. FSC-certified wood comes from forests that are harvested sustainably (i.e., more trees aren't taken down than can grow back, and there's minimal harm to the ecosystem).

Take an ecofriendly seat (or table, or bed):
Ecofriendly furniture is getting easier and easier to find and hopefully will soon be the norm. Crate & Barrel (crateandbarrel.com) has some eco pieces made from FSC-certified wood, with seat cushions filled with soy-based foam, back cushions made from postconsumer recycled fibers, and fabric treated with water-based products. The fabric isn't yet organic, but this is still decent for the mainstream. Any furniture that claims to be ecofriendly should be free of the fire-retardant chemicals PBDEs (described in the mattress section of this chapter on page 54), formaldehyde-free (formaldehyde is a volatile organic compound and carcinogen that's found in particle board and other compressed woods, including some plywood—if wood is formaldehyde-free, the manufacturer will know it and be proud of it), and free of toxic glues and finishes that off-gas VOCs. Ideally upholstered furniture features sustainable fabrics such as organic cotton, hemp, linen, or bamboo, too.

Give it away: If you're getting rid of furniture, don't send it to the dump. You once considered it nice (or at least serviceable)—someone else might, too. Like, say, a recent grad with a new apartment and no money (who will be eternally grateful and might be coerced into doing menial labor for you at some point). Don't know anyone like that? Ask around, put it on Freecycle.org or Craigslist, or donate it to a shelter or housing project. Good karma is good for your personal environment. Snicker if you will, but I think it's true. Anyway, it can't hurt.

DON'T ROLL OUT THE RED (WALL-TO-WALL) CARPET

Or any other shade of wall-to-wall carpet, for that matter. They're impossible to clean thoroughly, even if you steam them (and how often do you do that?), so they accumulate buckets of such tracked-in delicacies as soot, fungus, flea eggs, dust mite poop, arsenic, mercury, and traces of pesticides. Yum.

New carpet might be "cleaner" but it's not so good for you. With conventional wall-to-wall, the adhesive and padding are loaded with VOCs like toluene, formaldehyde, and xylene—all toxic to the nervous system. That new carpet smell is all those VOCs off-gassing. A lot of VOCs seep out during a carpet's first month or so in a home, and though the levels subside somewhat, those VOCs are as persistent as that certain someone you hooked up with *one* time in college who didn't stop calling you till three years after graduation. They never really go away.

Before the carpet arrives *chez vous*, it has to be manufactured. Chances are it was made from either nylon or olefin, both synthetic petroleum-derived fibers. Say it with me: Petroleum is a nonrenewable resource. And tons of that oil is wasted. Literally. More than 2 million tons of carpeting gets discarded (no, *not* recycled) in a year. Oh, and let's just say you don't want to drink the wastewater from a carpet factory: It's bursting with juicy chemicals from the dyeing and finishing processes.

What to do? Enjoy your bare floors if you've got 'em. They probably look sweeter than synthetic w-to-w. (But by the way, if you have carpeting all over the place, don't sweat it—just don't replace it with *new* carpeting when you get sick of it. Install some sustainable hardwood floors—maybe bamboo, maybe reclaimed wood—instead.) Throw down small area rugs (made from untreated natural fibers with no nasty glue) that you can shake out and maybe wash from time to time. If you really want the cushiness of carpet, buy it from a company like Interface (interfaceinc.com), which includes at least some renewable and recycled materials in its products, and sells carpet in tiles, thereby reducing waste (because you can buy exactly what you need, and not have to trim and trash any of it).

PAINT PROPERLY 🖋

If you're painting walls or furniture, use ecofriendly paints. Opt for low- or zero-VOC latex paint or milk-based paint rather than petroleum based paints.

Painting is an easy way to make a space look fresh, change a room's vibe dramatically, or vent suppressed rage. (I have a friend who always repaints her bedroom after a breakup.) But standard home paints contain volatile organic compounds that can off-gas—that is, be emitted into the air in the form of toxic gases—especially as the paint is being applied and while it's drying.

Common VOCs in paints include formaldehyde, toluene, and benzene. Newly painted rooms can have as much as one thousand times more VOCs than outside air, and a fresh coat off standard paint gives off more VOCs than any other indoor home product. Beyond that, the process of manufacturing petroleum-based paint produces ten times the weight of the paint in toxic waste. Ecofriendly paint is available at most hardware stores these days, and it's not much more expensive than regular yucky paint. Benjamin Moore produces a mass market line of low-VOC paints called Eco Spec, and BioShield (bioshield.com) offers a large selection of ecofriendly paints and finishes that are available in home stores all over the country. My favorite kind of paint is milk paint from Old Fashioned Milk Paint (milkpaint.com).

Save unused paint for future touch-ups (so you don't have to buy more) or donate it—a local shelter or nursing home might be psyched to get free paint (and of course yours is in a chic shade) so they can give their facility a little love—but don't dump it down the drain or in the trash.

Tip: Before you paint something a fresh shade, you may need to remove the crumbling, cracking, or fading paint that's already there. The easy way is chemical paint strippers. Typical paint strippers contain methylene chloride (also known as dichloromethane). You don't want this stuff near your person—inhaling its fumes may cause nausea, dizziness, skin irritation, burns, and eye irritation and may mess up your hand-eye coordination. (And then how will you paint?) With longer term exposure it's been linked to heart and lung problems, and it's a possible carcinogen. So look for strippers free of methylene chloride. If you're removing lead-based paint, ask a pro for help—you do not want to breathe in lead dust. At all.

BE WISE ABOUT WALLPAPER

If you're putting up wallpaper, always choose the vinyl-free kind.

Wallpaper? you ask.

There are lots of chic wallpaper options out there these days. (It's not your grandmother's wallpaper, okay?) I generally prefer painted walls to those adorned with patterned paper, but in a little space like a powder room (um, not that I *have* a powder room) a bold design can be a lot of fun.

Problem is, most wallpaper is made with vinyl (also known as PVC). Vinyl sucks. (This is another one of those "if you only take a few things away from this book . . ." proclamations.) As noted in the Plastics Primer on page 41, the production of vinyl is extremely energy-intensive and it releases dioxins into the environment. It off-gasses plasticizers (which are known endocrine disruptors and probably carcinogens) into your home—and releases more into the environment if it's discarded to a landfill. If it's burned, it releases more dioxins. (Bad, bad dioxins.) And depending on how much you use, wallpaper could be the biggest PVC item inside your home. So go vinyl-free.

Style bonus: Eliminating vinyl from consideration means a de facto ruling out of a whole lot of hideous wallpapers.

Digging deeper, try to pick a pattern that isn't printed using toxic heavy-metal-filled inks. The Boston-based design company Mod Green Pod (modgreenpod.com) makes fabulous ecofriendly wallpaper (as well as organic cotton textiles) that will look smokin' in your powder room. If you have one.

Chapter Four

DINING AND DRINKING

love to eat. Wait, I take that back. Most of the time I love to eat. When I have an amazing meal made from fresh ingredients prepared with love (or better, stellar kitchen skills), I am a really, really happy camper. However, when I scarf down a package of grocery store cookies that don't even taste good, I feel stuffed and guilty. That kind of eating I do not love.

Here's the great thing: Eating in a way that's truly pleasurable —with local, organic ingredients and minimal processed crapola—is the best way to eat for the environment. Something that's good for you and the planet is actually the most delicious. It's like a hall pass. Enjoy.

What does the food we eat (and the wine we drink) have to do with the environment? A lot—far more than I realized when I first started working on this book.

The food industry uses almost 20 percent of the energy consumed in the United States. Of that, 40 percent goes to process, package, and distribute food. Another 40 percent is used to refrigerate and cook it (the bulk of that is industrial, by the way). Which means only 20 percent is used to grow the ingredients—and half of *that* goes to producing and applying chemicals (fertilizers and pesticides).

Hopping up on my soapbox for a second: The industrial agriculture industry in this country is making a big stinking mess of the land and the water and the environment. Okay, I'm now off the soapbox. The good thing is that we (you and me, sweet pea) can actually do something about this. Without consumers buying into it, our giant food system can't function. So let's start making things change. (I feel like there should be some '60s war protest song playing right now. Sing one to yourself, please.) Even if you think your actions won't make a difference, collectively, they can. And at the very least, eating green tastes terrific and is better for you.

EAT LOCAL FOODS

No, I'm not the first one to come up with this idea. You've probably heard it before—eco-peeps and foodie types talk about it constantly. I can personally vouch for the fact that local ingredients—excuse me while I do the food-as-poetry thing for a moment—like a bright red tomato just off the vine and still warm from the sun, or tender spring greens dressed delicately with a splash of olive oil and a sprinkle of sea salt, or juicy peaches picked in the morning and baked in a pie in the afternoon taste orders of magnitude better than mealy, out-of-season produce and foods processed so much that you can't even tell what's in them.

The average food item travels about 1,500 miles before it arrives on your plate. When you buy locally produced food (from a farm stand or farmers' market or a store that stocks local produce), it travels an average of 50 miles. So your food from elsewhere uses thirty times more energy and results in the emission of thirty times more CO_2 into the atmosphere. And that's just transportation—food that's shipped also has to be packaged and refrigerated. A box of lettuce (not even a complex processed food) that travels from Cali to the East Coast requires almost sixty times more energy than is actually *in* the lettuce.

The farther produce travels, the longer the time from picking to eating, and the less healthy it is. That box of lettuce for your nutritious salad loses about 50 percent of its vitamin C within twenty-four hours of being picked and 50 percent of its flavanols (those cancer- and heart-disease-fighting things) if it's en route for a week. Local food tastes better, because it doesn't lose flavor while you're waiting for it. Plus, and possibly most importantly, buying locally supports the local economy and small farmers who—generally speaking—are careful with the land, who are more likely to use sustainable farming methods, and who grow many crops instead of just churning out hundreds of acres of one item (which is what big factory farms tend to do). The multi-crop thing is biodiversity, baby, and without it the soil becomes depleted of nutrients and needs more and more pesticides to grow anything.

Okay. So perhaps you're on board with the idea of trying to eat locally. Now you need a plan. At least I did. Amorphous suggestions like "eat locally" don't stick with me unless I establish concrete rules. Some people—and I admire them—follow the rule that they can only eat food that comes from within a certain radius, like 100 or 200 miles, of where they live. Amazing, but impractical for most of us.

Simply being aware that local is the best, the best for you, and the best for the environment will probably make you look for it more. But try this: Make sure you include at least one local food in your diet every day. This isn't so hard. It's really easy in the summer, when no matter where you live there's great produce growing locally. (During those times of year, try to eat five or ten local things every day). During less abundant times, you can have milk (and cheese and butter) from a local dairy, local eggs, preserves and pickles made from local ingredients, honey from local beekeepers . . . you get the idea. And it's fun to find out what's available near you—the more you ask about it, the more options you'll learn about it. And the more you request it where you shop, the more readily available local food will become.

Chic bonus: Knowing where your food comes from is so hot right now. Foodies love to chat about it. If you're having people over for dinner, being able to tell them where the goat cheese is made and which farm the mixed greens are from (*if* they're interested—there's a fine line between food connoisseur and obnoxious know-it-all, so don't cross it) guarantees raves. So does having delicious food, which is much easier when the ingredients are local and fresh.

Tip: *Talk* to the farmers at the farmers' market and the owners of food stores that carry local products. It's fun to hear from people who are passionate about this stuff, and you'll learn a lot that will impress your foodie friends.

SUPPORT SUSTAINABLE RESTAURANTS

Eat at restaurants that buy ingredients from local farms and make efforts to conserve energy and water and cut down on waste. Those are probably gonna be the best restaurants anyway, so this isn't a hard one. And it's worth doing: The restaurant industry represents 10 percent of the U.S. economy. A piece of the pie that big turning green—not in the moldy way—could make a huge difference to the environment. Running a restaurant can be a drain: Restaurants use 33 percent of the electricity in the retail sector, and an average restaurant uses 300,000 gallons of water per year. On the other hand, one restaurant can keep a small farm in business. Talk to the owners of your favorite restaurants to find out what they're doing in the name of sustainability—and if the answer is "nothing," ask them to start. Become a regular at the most sustainable restaurants in your city (being a regular at a sweet restaurant is definitely chic). Check out the Green Restaurant Association's website (dinegreen.com) to see what restaurants aren't just saying they're going green, but are actually getting certified. And see page 188 for a few of my personal favorite eco-eateries around the country.

Get it to go

Takeout food is a fabulous invention. When you're working hard or exhausted, you can have your food and eat it, too. Or something like that. While finishing this book, I got takeout every night. (Bad environmentalist!) Takeout is not so ecofriendly. Think about all the packaging. The plastic utensils. The zillion napkins they give you when you get one freaking salad. But you can make it better. When you place your order, request no bag, no napkins, and no utensils. Definitely no chopsticks. Ask twice—they don't always pay attention. If it's a place you know, try bringing your own reusable container. I'm not sure if they're supposed to, but my fave neighborhood joint throws my usual in there for me. And try to find places that are using more ecofriendly takeout containers—such as boxes made from 100 percent recycled content or utensils made from polylactic acid, a corn-based plastic. The Green Restaurant Association (dinegreen.com) has a growing list of takeout places offering less offensive packaging—and you could always ask your favorite place to make a change. Whatever you do, do not get your food in Styrofoam. (If you forget why, see page 43.)

Tip: Need a pizza fix? Pick up a frozen AmericanFlatbread (americanflatbread.com) at your local Whole Foods or another grocery store. No kidding, these things are unbelievably good (and they take, like, six seconds to heat up). And the company uses organic ingredients, and has regional bakeries around the country to cut down on the environmental damage caused by shipping foods long distances.

EAT ORGANIC FOODS

Eco types love to debate whether it's more important to eat local foods or organic foods. As you might guess from the fact that I put my local food rant closer to the beginning of the chapter, I'm in the choose-local-first camp, because much organic food—that's food grown without the use of chemical pesticides and fertilizers—comes from big industrial farms that are doing as much processing and packaging as conventional food producers, edging out smaller farmers, and shipping their products all over the world (and expending tremendous amounts of energy to do so).

But organic ingredients—especially when they are produced on a smaller scale—are fabulous. They're grown without synthetic fertilizers, pesticides, hormones, and antibiotics, meaning they're safer and healthier, and that growing them is better for the soil, groundwater, and atmosphere. They also require about 50 percent *less* greenhouse gas-emitting energy to grow than conventional foods, thanks to fertilizer- and pesticide-making processes and the transportation of grain to feed animals at factory farms.

Chemical fertilizers and pesticides are derived from petroleum (yep, that nonrenewable resource) in energy-intensive processes. Farms that grow only one crop—that's called monoculture, and it's basically the opposite of biodiversity, which is a healthy thing—end up with soil devoid of nutrients. So they need to keep dumping more fertilizers on their crops, and those crops miss out on all the nutrients that exist in organically farmed soil, instead just sucking up nitrogen, phosphorus, and potassium (periodic table symbols N, P, and K) that are in the fertilizers. Sure, N, P, and K make plants grow, but not especially healthy plants.

Runoff from pesticides and fertilizers, which contain neuro-toxins, carcinogens, skin and eye irritants, endocrine disrup-tors, and sometimes sewage (tasty!), and contaminates nearby groundwater. (Wait, you might be thinking . . . are all those tasty chemicals and that sewage getting on my food? Yup.) And when excess nitrogen-based fertilizers evaporate, they release nitrous oxide, a greenhouse gas. Converting one acre of farmland from conventional to organic could eliminate anywhere from 10 to 200 pounds of chemical pesticides and hundreds of pounds of chemical fertilizer from being used each year.

The ideal, naturally, is local *and* organic. But many small local farms that do practice truly organic methods aren't certified organic, because they don't have the resources required to get certified. If you go to a farmers' market, don't rule out produce that's not labeled organic. Ask the person at the stand what kind of pesticides they use—chances are good they steer clear of chemicals as much as possible.

Bottom line: Try to buy local organic foods when you can, opt for local stuff over processed organic from huge companies—I'll take locally made granola over organic Frosted Flakes, please—and when your food is coming from afar, organic is a far better choice.

Organic shopping list

Buying organic can be pricier, so here's a rundown of the produce items that have the most pesticides when grown conventionally— and come to you most contaminated. There are a few different versions of this list out there, so you may have read one with some different items on it. But in general, if you're going to go organic with any fruits and veggies, I'd suggest starting with these, which tend to be thinner skinned and more likely to absorb chemicals.

Strawberries

Bell peppers

Spinach

Grapes

Peaches

Nectarines

Celery

Apples

Apricots

Green beans

PUT DOWN THE PROCESSED CHEESE PUFFS

Choose whole, recognizable foods that are as close to their natural state as possible instead of refined foods—especially avoiding "foods" filled with long lists of ingredients you can't pronounce and that come from some mysterious, chemical-ridden, far away industrial source.

Admittedly, I've been known to enjoy a Ho-Ho or Yum-Yum snack cake fresh from its plastic wrap as much as the next gal. But you know what? It just ain't good for me. (And honestly, even if it tastes yum-yum in the moment, it never leaves me feeling especially perky.) It's not good for the environment, either.

Refining food strips away natural nutrients, which are basically replaced with more super-refined sugars and fats and really nothing good. And whereas normal (organic) food uses energy from sunlight—an unlimited resource—to grow, manufacturing processed foods requires mad crazy amounts of energy from petroleum. Just growing corn at a factory farm (in its various forms, factory-farm-grown corn is the primary ingredient in most processed foods, often as high-fructose corn syrup) takes 50 gallons of oil per acre. And that's just to *grow* the stuff. You still gotta turn it into that Yum-Yum cake.

You might wonder if the nutrients added back to food make up for some of the good stuff lost during the refining process. Well, somewhat. Eating a Yum-Yum cake with fortified flour is marginally better for you than eating a Yum-Yum cake with no vitamins. I guess. But having an apple or a salad or something is better. Besides, those added-back vitamins are created via an elaborate, energy-intensive manufacturing process that requires petroleum and dangerous chemical solvents and results in plenty of chemical waste.

Niacin, for example (and it's just one of many), is made by heating and pressurizing petroleum into methane, ethylene, and hydrogen. Meanwhile, air is liquidified (yeah, I have no idea how you do that) and separated into nitrogen and oxygen to make ammonia, then combined with hydrogen to make nitric acid. Then you stir up the ethylene and acetylene (which you got when you squeezed the petroleum into the methane, obviously) with water and platinum under pressure to get acetaldehyde, which is tossed with some of the ammonia from before. Add to that some of that nitric acid you made earlier and presto! You have niacin.

Or you could just eat an egg. (You know, an organic one.) That's a good source of niacin, too.

Probably the most important reason to say no to processed foods is that whole foods are simply healthier. Way healthier. The nutritious compounds that occur naturally in foods don't do the same tricks if they're extracted and fooled around with and reinjected into something so refined it's unrecognizable. And your body isn't designed to digest things like high-fructose corn syrup and synthetic sweeteners. So don't ask it to. And don't ask the environment to withstand so much stress just so you can have a Yum-Yum cake.

Green women don't get fat, part I

The obesity epidemic in the U.S. is getting worse every year, and there's a big correlation between that and the number of processed foods available to us. (There are seventeen thousand new food products on the market every year.) This isn't a diet book, but here's the thing: If you eat a green diet—that is, a diet based mainly on fresh, seasonal fruits and vegetables and involving almost no processed foods (from sugary cereals to baked goods to frozen dinners to margarine)—you probably aren't going to get fat. So you won't ever have to follow some convoluted diet du jour and keep track of how many carbs or fat grams or carrot sticks you're eating. How nice is that?

DRINK ORGANIC AND BIODYNAMIC WINES

Remember how I gave you that list of foods to buy organic? Remember how grapes were on it? Um, those are the same grapes that go into wine. So drink wine made from organically or biodynamically farmed grapes.

How does it taste? Glad you asked. Several months ago I bought my first bottle of organic wine. It was a 2005 viognier from Bonterra Vineyards in Mendocino, California. I'm actually surprised that I'd never intentionally tried organic wine before. Suffice it to say I like my wine. A lot. And I'm not particularly discriminating about what I'll try. (In college I lived off campus my senior year, and my roommates and I frequently threw dinner parties and served wine from a box. Come to think of it, we always had boxes o' wine in the fridge. And we went through them at a fairly rapid clip. Ah, Franzia.) Having said that, I do taste and write about wine fairly often for work, so I've developed a decent palate.

I chose this viognier because it was the only organic wine available at the store near my apartment. Fear not: This trend is changing, and more and more mainstream stores are carrying a wider selection of organic wines, although for now—unless you go to a wine store that specializes in organic bottles—you're likely to find only a handful of choices per store. They're fairly reasonably priced, though. The viognier I bought was $15.99, the same price as the bottle of non-organic sauvignon blanc I bought as well (admittedly, just in case I didn't like the organic stuff). When I checked wine.com, the range of prices for organic wines was $8.99 to $34.99. At Mare, a chi-chi restaurant that won a Best of Boston award from *Boston* magazine (and features lots of organic food and wine), the organic wine prices are right in line with the other bottles on the list, ranging from $32 on up to $120 (that includes the restaurant markup, of course). Drinking organic wine won't break the bank.

Quick confession: I'm drinking wine made from organic grapes as I write this, so forgive me if I ramble. I'm drinking in the interest of authentic research, you understand.

Organic grapes are those grown without artificial fertilizers or organic chemicals. Which means none of that stuff is getting into the air, water, or soil. Organic grape growers have to plant a variety of crops in order for their grapes to thrive, which is good because biodiversity leads to healthier soil. Basically, the more organic vineyards there are, the better for the planet. To be labeled 100 percent organic, wine has to be made from, yes, 100 percent organically produced ingredients. To be called organic, it needs to be made from at least 95 percent organically produced ingredients. And wines with at least 70 percent organically produced ingredients can say on their labels that they are "made with organic ingredients."

Back to the viognier. This can be a finicky grape varietal even when it's grown conventionally. It's fairly susceptible to mildew in humid conditions, and in order to get the right flavor from it, it has to be harvested at the perfect time. That's hard to do.

When it's good, though, viognier is one of my favorite white wines: rich, aromatic, a little flowery. But it's very often average or below. So this was a risky kind of wine to try for my first organic.

The Bonterra organic was not the best viognier I've ever had, but was good. It's fresh tasting; fruity but not sweet. Would I order this particular wine in a restaurant? Sure. Have I tried more organic or biodynamic wine? You betcha—it's almost all I drink now. Biodynamic farmers are actually more stringent in many ways than organic farmers. I visited Grgich Hills (a biodynamically farmed vineyard in Napa, California, that makes kick-ass wine—it's on some of the best wine lists in the country) and learned how the system works. It's a little complicated, but so safe and healthy and pesticide-free. They make "teas" from herbs such as chamomile to keep pests away and grow legumes next to the vines to add nutrients to the soil. It works, and you can eat the sugar snap peas straight off the vine—no washing necessary. I know. I did it.

A few other things to note: Some organic wines are produced with no added sulfites, which purportedly lessens the hangover effect. But many wines made with organically grown grapes do have sulfites, to protect the wine's flavor. Some people complain that uncorked organic wine doesn't last as long as regular wine—but really, you shouldn't have opened bottles of any kind sitting around for more than a couple days. And why on earth would you want to? You should be able to keep an open bottle of organic white in the fridge for three to four days and an open bottle of organic red on the counter for two.

With organic wine, as with all wine, you should drink what you like. If you don't like the first one you try, try another! (Really—if you tried, I don't know, a chardonnay that you didn't love, would you swear off chardonnay for the rest of your life? Come on . . . what would you drink at weddings?)

If you want to support the organic and biodynamic wine industries, buy it and drink it as often as you can and want to— and definitely order it if you spot one you know you like on a menu at a restaurant. While you're at it, let the server or the owner know you're happy it was there.

Ten terrific wineries

I've tasted many more organic wines since that first bottle of viognier—all in the interest of quality research, of course. Here are ten wineries that I think put out consistently excellent organic or biodynamic products. What's the point of drinking wine just because it's organic if it doesn't taste good? These wineries all sell bottles with price tags that don't frighten me (generally in the $8 to $50 range). If your wine store doesn't carry any of these, ask what they do have—many wineries in France and other European countries make organic products but don't really advertise the fact.

1. Larmandier-Bernier, Champagne, France

If going green meant I had to give up champagne, it might be a lost cause. But I don't, because this organic house makes supremely crisp, dry bubbles. Wow, is their stuff good.

2. Privat Laieta, Sant Sadurni D'Anoia, Spain

On a recent trip to Spain I became obsessed with cava. An inexpensive sparkling wine that tastes just like champagne? Yeah, I couldn't give that up, either—luckily, Privat Laieta makes an outstanding organic version.

3. Robert Sinskey Vineyards, Napa, CA

Very chic, with a gourmet bent, this winery produces a spectrum of delicious wines, from pinot blanc to cabernet sauvignon. robertsinskey.com

4. Frog's Leap Winery, Rutherford, CA

I liked Frog's Leap before I started this whole going-green process (without realizing they were organic), because even though they take wine seriously they never take themselves seriously. Frog's Leap makes a fantastic rosé (so hot right now), and they aren't afraid to call it "pink." frogsleap.com

5. Brick House Vineyards, Newberg, OR

Everyone is obsessed with pinot noir. It's especially cool to drink pinot from Oregon's Willamette Valley. And if that pinot is organic and tastes amazing—like Brick House's—that's as cool as it gets. brickhousewines.com

6. Quivira Vineyard, Heraldsburg, CA

Biodynamic wine (awesome sauvignon blanc, zinfandel, and rosé) from Dry Creek Valley in Sonoma. quivirawine.com

7. Grgich Hills, St. Helena, CA

My current favorite brand of wine. The guys running the show here are serious about wine and passionate about the environment—they're even running on solar energy. grgich.com

8. Jasper Hill, Victoria, Australia

Are you over wines from Cali and Europe? "Newer" wine regions like Australia do organic too, of course. If you tend to like Aussie shiraz, you'll probably think Jasper Hill's is sublime.

9. Château de Beaucastel, Rhone Valley, France

This proudly French and proudly all-natural winery makes awesome—some collection-worthy—reds and whites. beau-castel.com

> **10. Bonterra Vineyards, Ukiah, CA**
> Yup, this is the Mendocino Valley winery that made the viognier I
> described drinking. I've since tried their chardonnay, their syrah,
> and their merlot. All very good, and really reasonably priced.
> bonterra.com

A GOOD COLD ONE

When picking up a six-pack, remember that beer is made from
hops and barley and sometimes wheat. Conventionally, these
ingredients are grown with herbicides, insecticides, and especially
fungicides (hops are vulnerable to fungus). But there are a growing
number of organic beers and beers made from organic ingredients
out there (it was about a $20 million segment of the beer industry
in '05), and some are really good, such as Peak Organic (peak-
brewing.com) and Butte Creek (buttecreek.com). If you want to
save the energy used to transport heavy bottles of beer, support
local microbreweries. My favorite beer made in Massachusetts
comes from Nantucket's Cisco Brewers (ciscobrewers.com).
Nothing beats a cold Sankaty Light with a twist of lemon on a
summer day. They didn't pay me to say that, I swear.

COFFEE BREAK

Only drink coffee that is shade-grown, Fair Trade–certified, and
organic. That might sound high-maintenance, but it's actually
easy to find these days. Most food stores carry at least one if not

several brands—look for Green Mountain Coffee's (greenmountaincoffee.com) Fair Trade & Organic House Blend or Organic French Roast, Pura Vida (puravidacoffee.com), and the Organic Coffee Company (organiccoffeecompany.com). Certified organic and fair trade coffee will be clearly labeled. And yes, you can get it at Starbucks. Phew.

Why bother? I've known, vaguely, for a long time that we should care about saving the rainforests. And recently I found out why: Coffee trees' natural habitat is in the shade, under the canopy of the rainforest. (I think I read that last part somewhere—sorry to cop the words, but doesn't it sound lovely?)

But a few decades ago coffee farmers found that you could grow coffee a lot faster if you cleared away the lovely canopy and grew coffee in the sun. So they were just cutting down rainforests, and I *know* you're not supposed to do that. And I've learned why: Because clearing and burning rainforests emits CO_2, methane, and nitrous oxide; because rainforests are the natural habitat of more than half of the plant and animal species in the world; and because rainforests—which used to cover about 15 percent of the planet and have been deforested to the point where they now cover only about 7 percent of the planet—absorb tons of CO_2 and help slow global warming. Sweet, those rainforests.

Yet another problem with growing coffee in the sun is that the only way it can grow year after year is if it's doused with pesticides (take a plant out of its natural conditions and it generally needs chemical help). *Most* of the pesticides are burned away when the coffee is roasted, but they're doing damage to the people who live in the regions where coffee is grown (especially the workers on sun-grown coffee plantations) and further damaging local ecosystems.

Organic coffee is grown with no pesticides, and that means it probably had to be grown in the shade, too. If you like decaf, the organic certification ensures that methylene chloride—the chemical I suggest you avoid in *paint strippers*—wasn't used to remove the caffeine.

Fair Trade–certification isn't necessarily directly linked to the environment, but it assures that coffee growers are getting a fair price for their product and that workers are getting a fair wage and aren't subjected to dangerous and cruel working conditions (the coffee growing world has been associated with some bad practices—but that could take up a whole separate book. Hmmm, maybe the next one).

Tea, honey?

Try to drink organic tea, too. Nonorganic tea growers use a lot of pesticides, including some (such as DDT) that have been banned in the U.S. My friend Amie sent me a bunch of different kinds of organic tea from Stash (stashtea.com) to keep me awake while I was finishing this book. It's really good. Choice Organic Teas (choiceorganicteas.com) has a killer selection of white, black, and green teas and offers many teas in loose-leaf form, which means less packaging, which is always a good eco-thing. Organic teas from The Republic of Tea (republicoftea.com) are widely available and come in bulk loose leaf form, too. While you're at it, sweeten that tea with honey from a local beekeeper. Bees, those busy, buzzy little pollinators, are critical to the growth of fruit and flowers. The bee population in the United States declined dramatically in 2007, and though (at the time I'm writing this) no one is quite sure why, some scientists think global warming could be to blame. A professor of fruit science I talked to—who knew they had those?—said small beekeeping operations may help to sustain bee populations. And you already know why buying local food is so nice.

GO FISH

Buy and order fish carefully. This is kind of a complicated one. You could stop eating fish altogether, but fish can be super-healthy and so delicious that it would be mean to suggest giving them up. If you want to keep eating fish, here's what you should know.

A combination of overfishing, pollution, development, and global warming is threatening fish species and fish habitats, from oceans to streams, all over the world. The lists of specific fish to avoid and fish that are ok to eat changes frequently. It's not just the species, either. How they're raised (farmed or wild—I guess if they're wild they're not really being raised, but you know what I mean) and how they're caught (line-caught or trapped or dragged) and where they come from matters, too. And then there are the contaminants—many fish contain mercury and polychlorinated biphenyls (PCBs) that are potentially harmful, especially if you're preggers or a kid.

I know I'm not making this much easier for you, but here are a few rules to follow. At least for now.

- If you want salmon, opt for wild Pacific or Alaskan salmon. Farmed salmon tends to be high in pollutants and sadly low in flavor; wild Atlantic salmon is a protected species.
- When you're expecting, steer clear of fish high in mercury such as sea bass, swordfish, Atlantic halibut, tuna . . . actually, talk to your doc about what to avoid and be cautious, okay? Don't panic if you have a bite accidentally, but don't order it every week as an entrée, either.
- Wild salmon, sardines, squid, Arctic char, and Atlantic fluke are the lowest-mercury fish.
- Avoid farmed shrimp, especially imported farmed shrimp, which is associated with high levels of pollutants that damage wild fish populations and degradation of mangrove forests. Also avoid shrimp caught by net-dragging (for every pound of shrimp caught, there are up to 15 pounds of bycatch, or other sea creatures such as sea turtles, killed).
- Carry a seafood information card, like the one available from the Audubon Society at seafood.audubon.org, and have it on hand for those times when you're feeling fishy.
- Think of fish more like you think of produce and eat it only when it's in season near you. For example, mackerel swims up the eastern seaboard and passes by Boston in late May or so. That's a darn good time to eat mackerel in Boston, and it's the only time sustainability-minded Boston chefs will have it on the menu. You can't always get what you want, my friend, but if you try sometimes you just might find . . . that patience makes a good thing taste even better.
- Ask questions! Find out where your fish came from, if it's being harvested sustainably, what levels of mercury and PCBs it contains,

and how it was caught. If your waiter or fishmonger doesn't know, say, "no, thank you."

. . . .

Tip: To help keep the habitats of wild salmon clean and safe, when you buy wine or produce from the Pacific Northwest, look for items certified salmon-safe by an organization cleverly named Salmon-Safe (salmonsafe.org).

EAT LESS MEAT

Although it's true that the first bite of a perfect hamburger straight off the grill can be a little bit of heaven in a bun, we all *need* to eat less meat. I'm not saying we need to give it up entirely, but we need to cut way, way back and think of it as a special treat. And when we enjoy that special treat, we should get it from a small, local farm where cows roam in a pasture and feed on grass.

The average American eats more than 200 pounds of meat per year. That amount is environmentally costly. Producing a pound of beef can use more than 13,000 gallons of water. By comparison, it takes about 21 gallons of water to produce a pound of tomatoes. Adding insult to injury, livestock waste has polluted more than 27,000 miles of rivers. And talk about gassy: Between the methane emitted from cow farts and manure and the CO_2 emitted in transporting feed to farms and meat to consumers, producing one hamburger patty gives off as much greenhouse gas as a 6-mile car ride. It takes as much land to provide one person with a meat-based diet as it does to feed six people on a plant-based diet.

There are also health issues. Almost eighty million cases of food-related illness are reported in the United States each year, and meat from factory farms is involved with the majority of those. Cows on these farms are kept in such close proximity that wide-scale contamination could happen easily; they also feed on dead animals, including dead horses, pigs, and chickens. Even healthy cows are given antibiotics, the widespread use of which contributes to increasing bacterial resistance, and 80 percent of cows are injected with growth hormones, which poses a potential cancer risk to humans. Meat can also carry dioxins, the toxic chemicals that may cause cancer and disrupt the human endocrine system.

All righty then. Psyched for a steak? As I said, you don't have to give it up. But you should systematically and intentionally cut back. I don't know how much meat you eat, but if you eat it multiple times per week, try cutting back to once a week. If you have it once a week (that's about what I used to have), try scaling back to once every two weeks or once a month. That's about where I am now—being a food writer and trying new restaurants and recipes all the time, it's tough for me to rule anything out from my diet completely. Who am I kidding? Sometimes I just crave red meat.

Tip: Consider the source

"Consider the source" was one of my grandfather's favorite expressions. It's a great idea in life—before you trust an opinion or believe a rumor or buy something because the working-on-commission salesgal tells you it's *sooo* cute, think about who's saying it. It's a great idea with meat, too. When you do eat meat, always, always, always know where it comes from, and *insist* on meat that is grass-fed, organic (so none of the feed the cows ate was treated with chemical pesticides), hormone-free, antibiotic-free, and from a small, local farm. Good grocery stores may have this (and if they don't know what you're talking about when you ask, they don't have it), as will smaller natural food markets and specialty butchers. You could even—gasp—get it directly from a farm! Those kinds of cows do little, if any, damage to the environment and the meat is more nutritious and far less likely to make you sick.

LIKE ORGANIC FOR CHOCOLATE

So sorry, but you have to give up chocolate in all its forms immediately.

Wait, wait, I'm kidding. Man, if you saw the giant chocolate brownie I just inhaled, you would know how kidding I am. It was made with organic chocolate at a local bakery, but still . . . Damn, that thing was good.

You can definitely keep eating chocolate, but it'll be better if it's organic, and preferably fair trade. Like the plant that grows coffee beans, the cacao tree—the source of cocoa beans, from whence come all things chocolate—grows naturally in the shade and rainforest climate. In an attempt to grow more plants more quickly, cocoa farmers have started growing cacao trees in full sunlight (and cutting down rainforests to do it).

This might work for a little while, but it's not a sustainable way to grow cacao trees, because in the sun they are more susceptible to heat stress, disease, and pests. The answer? Use lots of chemical fertilizers and pesticides. (Wrong answer, but it's the one many farmers pick so they can meet demand.) Not only do the pesticides end up in the air and groundwater near cocoa farms, they are in the chocolate itself. Mmm . . . doesn't that chocolate-almond-insecticide bar sound luscious?

To ensure that your chocolate is free of chemical residues, buy only certified organic chocolate. To save the rainforest—don't you love that you can save the rainforest by eating chocolate? Look for shade-grown chocolate, ideally as certified by the Rainforest Alliance. Fair Trade certification is also an excellent thing to look for, because most Fair Trade chocolate happens to be organic and shade-grown, and you know the cocoa farmers who sold the beans got a fair price. Organic chocolate isn't hard to find—it's at most grocery stores and gourmet shops, and it's not much more expensive than conventional chocolate. If you can't find it near you, ask for it. These days I'm diggin' Dagoba (dagobachocolate.com), an Oregon-based chocolate company that makes bars, baking chocolate, and hot cocoa and is all about being organic and shade-grown.

SKIP SODA

There aren't many things I'm suggesting you quit cold turkey. Soda is one of them. Okay, maybe not *cold* turkey—if you want to have a small-batch artisinal root beer float every now and then, go for it. I'm talking about big-name vending machine soda.

Stop drinking it.

If you aren't hooked on the sody, no prob. If you are, this is a tough one. I know. I used to drink a Diet Coke every day. Sometimes three. I gave it up about a year ago, and the first couple of weeks were brutal. After that, though, I totally stopped craving it. I tried one a few months ago, and it didn't even taste that good—haven't had one, or been tempted to, since then. Right, I'll stop patting myself on the back now and say hey, good luck to you. Stick with it. Treat yourself to a massage or something when you make it through your first soft drink-free week.

Here are some reasons to think about becoming a quitter.

First, soda tends to come in either plastic bottles or aluminum cans. (I am a master of the obvious.) The production of both plastic and aluminum requires truckloads of energy. Or it would if energy came in trucks. Anyway, making a pound of aluminum emits about 12 pounds of CO_2, even more than making a pound of plastic (see page 15). Making recycled aluminum requires only about 5 percent of that energy, but in the United States we waste (throw away instead of recycle) more than fifty billion aluminum cans per year. If those had been recycled, that would have saved sixteen million barrels of crude oil—or enough energy to provide electricity for 2.7 million homes. Still, most soda cans contain more recycled content than soda bottles, which are starting to use recycled PET (#1) plastic, but only as a very small percentage. Oh, and both plastic bottles and soda cans leach bisphenol-A, a possible carcinogen and hormone disruptor. So don't sweat the can versus bottle decision too much—neither is good.

Then there's the energy required to make it the actual soda. If you drink full-strength sugary soda, all that sweetness comes from high-fructose corn syrup, one of the more energy-intensive ingredients to make. It takes more than ten times as much energy to make the high-fructose corn syrup as the energy actually *in* the syrup in the form of calories. (Incidentally, those are—as my mom would say—empty calories. Why blow calories on this junk when you could have dessert?) And then the fizzy, chemically soda has to be made, which is among the most energy-intensive food-making processes there is.

And *then* there's the other nasty stuff in soda, especially diet soda. Diet sodas with ascorbic acid and either sodium or potassium benzoate (a typical diet soda combo) can have little internal reactions that create benzene, a carcinogen. Nonsugar sweeteners such as aspartame and saccharine are also possible human carcinogens (they're proven carcinogens in rats, and what if a rat sips the remnants of your drink? Poor little rat). Think twice before you open a pop if you happen to be in India: Pesticide residues have been hanging out in certain major soda brands there for years, and a recent sampling discovered pesticide levels twenty-five to thirty times *higher* than they were in 2003.

Beauty bonus: I won't go too far into the diet and obesity implications of soda—but there are a lot of studies that say both sugary and calorie-free sodas can make you fat. And personally I think they're bad for your skin.

So my advice regarding soda is simple. It's back near the beginning of this section, but I'll put it down here again for symmetry: Stop drinking it.

PERUSE YOUR PACKAGING

When it comes to food packaging, less is more. No, really it's less—but that's better. About 50 percent of all municipal waste (that's the waste coming from you and me, not the big bad factories down the street) is discarded packaging. This is a big area where we need to *reduce*. As in, use less. (Ugh, okay, I'm going to do it: Remember that the three Rs of environmentalism are reduce, reuse, and recycle. Reduce comes first.) Besides, any food encased in layers of seemingly impenetrable packaging or wrapped in a convenient single serving size probably isn't so local, or non-processed, or organic.

Think about it this way: Single serving packages = bad. Bulk packaging = better (*if* you're actually going to consume what you buy and it's healthy). No packaging = best.

Most of all, avoid plastic packaging as much as you can. On page 41 I went over the different types of plastic, so you know to steer clear of numbers three, six, and seven. Problem is, a lot of food packaging plastic isn't labeled. Think about the clear plastic wrap around most grocery store meat. It's often our old foe number three—the dreaded vinyl, the evil PVC. But how would you know that? There's no number three on there. And then you don't know if you can recycle it, or which bin it should go into.

Plus, the production of all plastic is, as I've said before, incredibly energy-intensive—and not enough of it gets recycled. If you're choosing between two packaged products and need a tie-breaker, check what's in the packaging and *always* choose one made from recycled materials over one made from virgin materials. Choosing products made from recycled materials closes the recycling loop, creates a market for recycled stuff, and means what you're bringing home used less energy than it might have.

Tip: Once you've chosen your food-in-minimal-packaging, don't carry it home in grocery store shopping bags—not plastic or paper. I explain why on page 118. Bring your own bag(s), and that goes for the produce aisle and those rolls of clear plastic bags for carting home apples and grapes and such. You don't need 'em. You're washing your produce when you get home, right? If you really like those produce bags, save them when you get home and bring them back to the store to reuse.

Seven great items for setting a green chic table

When looking for goodies for your dining room, keep these eco-options in mind.

1. Riverside Design Group recycled glass plates (shopblue-house.com)
2. Transglass recycled glass jug and glasses (re-modern.com)
3. Esque recycled glass Italian carafe and wine tumblers (branchhome.com)
4. Viva Terra teak flatware (vivaterra.com)
5. Rawganique hemstitched organic hemp napkins (rawganique.com)
6. Bambu bamboo-handled cheese plane (shopbluehouse.com)
7. Bambu bamboo Chop, Scoop + Serve board (branchhome.com)

Chapter Five

HELLO, GORGEOUS

Many environmental types will tell you that the most ecofriendly beauty routine is no beauty routine at all—or at least, a beauty routine that involves no products from the cosmetics industry. I'm not one of those types. Hey, I'm not willing to give up the goods myself.

This chapter looks at a variety of personal care products and what's in them, ingredients to avoid if possible, and lots of healthy, earth-friendly alternatives. Don't be afraid, even if you're a beauty product junkie. Greening your beauty regimen—phasing out some eco-offenders and hazardous ingredients and incorporating natural, biodegradable products that are safe for you (and safe for the planet when they go down the drain)—can help you look and feel more gorgeous than ever.

Does that sound like a little too much hype? Thought so. Here's the deal: You can have a green(er) beauty regimen without sacrificing a bit of pretty, but only you will know what works for you and what you're comfortable with. And there is a good chance that becoming more conscious of what you're putting on your face and body, choosing healthier ingredients, and being aware of how important it is to take *care* of yourself will make you look better. (I could say who cares about that because it's what's on the inside that counts, but let's be real. We all want to look good.)

Before you go shopping, let me make one suggestion. Wait, two suggestions. First, read this chapter. Next, get in the habit of looking at labels carefully. The front of the package may shout "all-natural" or "hypo-allergenic" but that doesn't mean much. Most of the claims made on personal care packaging are unregulated and have no official definition.

Speaking of unregulated claims, you might figure that even if a package exaggerates its claims, it must be healthy because it's in a store, right? The government requires testing on all this stuff, right? Not so, cutie. You're on your own here. Less than 20 percent of personal care products have been tested for immediate adverse effects, and less than 10 percent have been tested for long-term, mutagenic, or reproductive effects. So pay attention. (I meant that in a nice, helpful way—not in a mean teacher way.)

RETHINK THE MANI-PEDI

I love having my toes pampered as much as the next gal— probably more. But the process of getting your nails done can be—if you think about it—a yucky, chemical-ridden process from start to finish. Those pedicure sinks with remnants of other people's skin and bacteria. Those shared tools. Those nonbiodegradable, toxic cleaners most spas and salons use.

And then there are the nail care products. Chemicals in products applied to the nails go straight to the bloodstream, via the skin, without passing through the liver. (I was surprised to learn that the nail doesn't provide much of a buffer—though it's hard, it's extremely absorbent.) Many polishes contain formaldehyde, which, as I've said, is a probable carcinogen along with its many other undesirable qualities, as well as dibutylphthalate. Yes, that is the word phthalate in there, which you've seen before. The dibutyl version is a potential reproductive toxin and endocrine disruptor, making it a particularly big no-no for moms-to-be. Nail polish also often contains the VOC toluene, a neurotoxin.

Another neurotoxin, acetate, is a common ingredient in nail polish remover. The bottle of nail polish remover I found in my bathroom proudly proclaims that it's "non-acetone." Acetone is a poison in many removers that takes off polish quite effectively but also can cause, according to the National Institutes of Health: death; coma; unconsciousness; seizures; respiratory distress; kidney damage; nose, throat, lung, and eye irritation; intoxication; headaches; fatigue; stupor; light-headedness; dizziness; confusion; increased pulse rate; nausea; vomiting; and shortening of the menstrual cycle in women. Whoa.

Okay, good for my bottle for being acetone-free. But the stuff I have sure does contain acetate (ethyl acetate, to be precise; other forms are amyl and butyl acetate). Plus, the back of the bottle tells me this is "extremely flammable. Liquid and vapors may ignite. Do not use when smoking. Do not use near fire, flame, or heat. Keep out of eyes. Harmful if ingested. Harmful to synthetic fabrics, wood finishes, and plastics." Hmmm. Sure, it's harmful to my fleece jacket and my coffee table, but I'm sure it's fine for me.

The point is: This stuff is not good. Lots of products that we think are safe are bad for our skin or our respiratory system or our insides. Read labels, read warnings, and be on the lookout for ingredients you know are toxic.

And if that doesn't give you pause, remember that when nail polish and nail polish remover go down the drain, they can seep into and contaminate groundwater—and they can also leach out of landfills. In other environmental news, yes, technically nail polish bottles are recyclable, but they almost never get recycled because there's dried up polish gunk left in there. Have you ever completely used up a bottle of nail polish? Me either. Ever thrown a half-full one in the trash? Me too.

Artificial nails are not a better choice. Personally I think they look slightly scary—but more importantly they harbor bacteria (so much so that they have been banned in some hospitals) and the juice used to get 'em off you is acetonitrile, which is similar to acetone—you don't want this stuff nearby. And you definitely don't want it near any kids.

Did I freak you out? Don't cancel your appointment yet. I still get pedicures. I have found places all over the country that don't have pedicure sinks but instead fill lovely glass or metal bowls with warm water for soaking my tootsies. (Check city and regional magazines or their websites, or DailyCandy

(dailycandy.com) to find one wherever you happen to be.) They reserve a set of tools for each client, and they use scrubs and lotions that I would use at home (with ingredients I've heard of and can pronounce, like sugar and cocoa butter). I skip polish entirely (it's an unnatural color that just gets chipped in a few days) and have my nails buffed to a pretty shine instead.

If you're dying for a vampy red or a flirty pink, *only* use brands that are free of toluene, phthalates, and formaldehyde, such as Spa Ritual (sparitual.com) and Firozé (firoze.com). Make sure the remover is acetone- and acetate-free, such as No Miss Vegan Nail Polish Remover. Although more and more salons offer safer polish options, the remover is harder to find. So I suggest taking your polish off at home pre-mani-pedi.

CARE FOR YOUR HAIR

Let's shake things up and go from toes to head. As my friend Meg always says, hair is the accessory you wear every day. So you want it to look good. I've been known to spend way, way, way too much money on shampoo and conditioner, and I think that's just fine. This is not a place to skimp.

And it's not a place to use toxic chemicals. Does it *really* matter what's in your shampoo and conditioner? It's just on there for a few seconds and then it washes off, right? As you probably guessed from the fact that I have a section on shampoo and conditioner, that's not totally true.

As I mentioned earlier, the chemicals in products applied to the skin go straight to the bloodstream without being detoxified by the liver. Hair is not skin, but scalp sure is, and it's thin skin at that. Thin skin that's made even more permeable by the steamy water of your shower and the detergent action of shampoos.

Some of the ingredients you don't want invading your scalp—but which are commonly present in shampoos—include:

- Formaldehyde, that old carcinogen we dislike so much, which acts as a preservative and sometimes goes by the name of quaternium-15
- Bronopol (a preservative that may also contain formaldehyde), which can react with triethanolamine (TEA) or diethanolamine (DEA) within the bottle to create nitrosamines, another carcinogen
- Parabens (methyl-, butyl-, propyl-, and ethyl-), which are hormone disruptors and have been linked with breast cancer
- Phthalates, which are often not listed as such because they are one of many ingredients in an added synthetic fragrance
- Coal-tar chemicals, carcinogens present in many synthetic FD&C and D&C colors
- Sodium laurel sulfate, which can harm the immune system, damage the eyes, and combine with other ingredients to form nitrosamines, which are carcinogens

Got all that?

There's more, but those are some of the big ones. And remember that in addition to assaulting you, all those funky chemicals are assaulting soil and groundwater when you rinse them off. Plus a lot of shampoos come in PVC bottles. I'm not going to issue another diatribe about PVC right now. Don't buy stuff that comes in it, 'kay?

Back to the ingredients. This is a lot to remember. You could carry this book around everywhere with you (then we'll always be together), or make a cheat sheet, or you could just look for shampoos that contain only ingredients you recognize and spell out their safety metrics in detail instead of making vague promises about being natural.

I warn you: As you peruse healthy shampoos (hey, that rhymes)—which you can find at health food stores, Whole Foods, and the organic section of most grocery stores, and which come in a whole range of prices from cheap to chi-chi—do sniff tests. They don't all smell fabulous. (Aside from looking fabulous, hair should definitely smell fabulous.) But some do, I promise! I am currently using the Vanilla & Sweet Orange Shampoo from Hugo (hugonaturals.com), which the label tells me specifically is "sulfate-free, cruelty-free and contains no parabens, petroleum products, animal fats, alcohols, or artificial colors or fragrances." From what I can tell the good smell comes from the vanilla extract, vanilla essential oil, and sweet orange essential oil listed among the ingredients (most of which I've heard of, by the way). I'm conditioning with Aubrey Organics' Honeysuckle Rose (aubrey-organics.com). The shampoos and conditioners from Burt's Bees (burtsbees.com) and John Masters Organics (johnmasters.com) are also terrific. And, okay, I know I'm not a kid anymore and clearly *not* the target audience, but Tween Beauty (tweenbeauty.com) makes Orange Sherbet Shampoo and Vanilla Bean Conditioner that smell a-maze-ing. I totally want to give some to all my BFFs. TTYL.

Shopping strategy: While you peruse the shampoos (I had to say it again because I like the rhyme so much), check out what the bottles are made of. I already mentioned PVC. Don't go there. Many companies (Burt's Bees is one) put as much postconsumer recycled content into their bottles as possible. If you have the choice, always opt for something recycled over something made from virgin plastic. Are you getting sick of me saying that yet?

Tip: The word "organic" isn't regulated in the cosmetics industry. So while buying products with organic ingredients is great (better for the earth; better for you), make sure they're *certified* organic. (The package will say so.) Or you might be paying extra for a whole lotta nothing.

SAVE YOUR FACE, PART I (SKINCARE PRODUCTS)

Many of the chemicals that star in shampoos make appearances in skincare products such as facial cleansers and moisturizers, too. And that's not the whole story.

Lots of lines feature ingredients derived from petroleum, which add moisture to the skin. You may see them listed as mineral oil, paraffin, or propylene glycol. Petroleum is a nonrenewable resource, but the big concern, facially speaking, is that these ingredients are likely culprits behind clogged pores. And blackheads. And zits. What's the point? In addition to avoiding the chemicals described in the shampoo and nail polish sections of this chapter, stay away from petroleum and petroleum-derived gunk.

I am currently loving the Juice Beauty skincare line, which is made with certified organic ingredients and free of pesticides, parabens, phthalates, petroleum . . . and some other bad stuff that doesn't start with P. Jāsön (jason-natural.com) is another obsession of mine. I've been using their Red Elements anti-oxidant line and my skin has never looked better.

Tip: The term "unscented" is unreliable. It may just mean some of the chemical smells from the product are masked with more chemicals, thus rendering the whole chemical mess aroma-neutral. With all beauty stuff, look for products labeled fragrance-free or, if you enjoy things that smell good, products with fragrance derived from truly natural sources such as essential oils. Avoid anything with the ambiguous ingredient "fragrance" listed, because it may contain formaldehyde, phthalates, and parabens.

High five

To simplify a little, here's a list of five common ingredients important to avoid in cosmetics—for you and for the planet. In handy alphabetical order. If you don't remember anything else, keep these in mind (and skip the artificial colors and artificial fragrances, too).

1. Formaldehyde
2. Parabens
3. Phthalates
4. Petroleum
5. Toluene

SAVE YOUR FACE, PART II (MAKEUP)

Because we need a little break from discussing unhealthy ingredients, let's start with something else. Packaging! Because of the way it's presented in precious little tubes and compacts with excessive layers and complicated component parts in plastic and metal all glued together and the fact that we almost never use up makeup products before tossing them, most makeup packaging is unrecyclable. Bummer.

There are a few innovative companies like Cargo (cargocosmetics.com) doing neat things with packaging—Cargo has a line of lipsticks called Plant Love with tubes made from corn and a box that you can plant and grow wildflowers. Seriously. So, that's all cool and we should let companies doing stuff like that know how shmantastic we think it is. (Alas, though the Cargo lippie is free of petroleum and other unfortunate additives, it does contain parabens. Why'd they play us like that?) Another option: Though your lipstick box won't grow a tree, Aveda (aveda.com) is consistently creative in their use of recycled materials for packaging. Their Lip Color Sheer, for example, comes in a tube made from 88 percent postconsumer recycled resin; the carton is made from 100 percent recycled newsprint, and you can buy refills instead of getting a whole new set of packaging each time.

Until all packaging is so thoughtfully designed, try to buy only makeup that *you're actually going to use*. No more impulse purchasing of some peachy blush when you know peach makes you look like a clown on a sugar high.

And we're done here.

Nope, can't let you off that easy. On to ingredients. Department store and drugstore brands of makeup, you may not be shocked to learn, often contain oodles of badness. Is that too judgmental? I don't know—the skin on your face is extremely sensitive and susceptible to chemicals.

Lipsticks are usually the worst offenders, and that stinks because you're putting them on your lips and over the course of your lifetime you may eat *pounds* of the stuff (4 to 9 pounds, to be exact). They are often petroleum-based and contain formaldehyde in the form of preservatives such as DMDM hydantoin, diazolidinyl urea, imidazolidinyl urea, and the afore-mentioned quaternium-15 and bronopol. What's a girl to do? Lavera (lavera.com) makes gorgeous lipsticks and glosses out of ingredients like shea butter and almond oil. Just thinking about it makes my lips softer.

In addition to the chemicals we've already discussed in this chapter, look out for lead (usually seen as lead acetate) in eye makeup, because it's a neurotoxin. Also avoid talc in eye shadow and face powder, because it's another carcinogen. Mercury, another potent neurotoxin, is sometimes found in trace amounts in eye makeup, too. You don't want that.

So I know this is a lot to take in and it's way too much to remember every time you shop for a beauty product. But if you start reading labels, you'll get a feel for which brands you can generally trust (think Ecco Bella, Aveda, Dr. Hauschka), and which are just too toxic.

Tip: Some cosmetic companies will take back their packaging for recycling. MAC offers a "Back to MAC" program—bring back six containers, get a free lipstick.

Shopping strategy: Powders, blushes, and eye shadows from many companies come in refillable compacts—ask if that's a possibility with your favorite brand.

Sunshine day

Did you see the *Brady Bunch* episode where Peter's voice changes? If so, sing the title of this sidebar to that tune. If not, forget I said anything. Moving on.

Your dermatologist begs you to wear sunscreen every day; you've heard it might be bad for you and the environment. Try to avoid sunscreens with parabens, DEA, and TEA (the ill effects of which I described earlier in this chapter) and opt for chemical-free sunblocks, or those that use titanium dioxide or zinc oxide as sunblock. Try Jāsön (jason-natural.com), California Baby (californiababy.com), or UV Natural (uvnaturalusa.com). And wear a big hat and shades, and stay out of the sun between ten and three, all right?

DISS THE DISPOSABLES

Choose your most disposable personal care products wisely. Most beauty products come with an inherent level of disposability, yes, but some things—toothbrushes and razors, for example—we absolutely *crank* through.

Fifty million pounds of toothbrushes wind up in landfills every year. I'm not suggesting you keep using the same toothbrush forever—dentists actually suggest changing your toothbrush four times per year, but on average Americans tend to change it less than half that often. Which, I guess, is good for the planet but maybe not so good for our teeth?

Minimize your impact by using a toothbrush that's not made from virgin plastic. Recycline's Preserve toothbrushes (recycline.com), for example, are made from 100 percent recycled #5 plastic. Which is good for two reasons: First, they aren't using virgin plastic. (As you might have guessed.) And second, they are providing an outlet for the eminently recyclable but hard-to-find-a-place-to-recycle-it #5.

Or throw away less each time you change your brush. Eco-Dent's Terradent toothbrush (eco-dent.com) comes with a permanent handle and changeable heads—so when it's time to change, you just throw away the bristly part and snap a new head into place and add less bulk to the landfill heap.

When you brush, I hope you're also flossing, young lady. Eco-Dent also makes an ecofriendlier floss that comes with 100 yards instead of the 30 or so you get with a lot of brands, and is packed in a minimal cardboard package—which is recyclable—instead of a plastic case.

Moving to razors, two billion disposable ones wind up in landfills every year. Cut way down by using a razor with a reusable handle and changing the blade. (Or, if you're really bold, a long-lasting straight razor, but I'm not going there. Electric razors are all plasticky and they use electricity and don't shave as close, so I don't suggest using those.) Even better if the reusable handle is made from recycled plastic, like Recycline's Preserve razor is. Will tried Preserve's Triple razor after a long weekend at his family's summer place in

Canada (where, I was told the first time I visited, showering is frowned upon if you want to be one of the boys . . . a swim in the lake is all you need). Needless to say, he hadn't shaved in three days. It worked like a charm, and he was a fan. Meanwhile, I tried it on my legs, which I hadn't shaved during the three days he was in Canada. It did the trick very well there, too.

By the way, Eco-Dent and Preserve both accept their products back to be recycled when you're done with them; they and other ecofriendly lines are available at Whole Foods and health food stores, and Preserve is now on shelves at Wal-Mart.

To shave or not to shave (while showering)

Some proponents of the environment advise shutting off the shower while soaping yourself up, turning it back on only to rinse. As I mentioned earlier, I enjoy my hot showers, and the idea of standing, dripping, and shivering myself into a lather doesn't appeal. However, one segment of my shower routine that I can remove from the spray is shaving my legs. (I still do my pits in the shower. I'm in there scrubbing them anyway, and it takes seven seconds per pit. I timed it this morning. I'm ok with that.) Depending on how careful and thorough I am, shaving my legs takes anywhere from thirty seconds to a minute apiece. Because every minute by which you reduce your shower time saves about 100 pounds of CO_2 per year, shaving my legs with a small bowl of water and the sink means 100 to 200 pounds less CO_2 from me.

> **Beauty bonus:** When I shave my legs out of the shower I'm definitely more thorough, and I have an easier time getting those spots I usually miss, like my knee. How is it that I so often miss an entire knee?

TALKING TAMPONS 🐚

Dealing with your monthly cycle may not be the most glamorous of topics, but, sweetie, it's hardly glamorous *not* to deal with it. Tampons aren't a beauty product per se, but they're about as personal as personal care products get.

Before I began researching this book, I was definitely a conventional tampon user.

Some books I read about being more ecofriendly (including one written by a man) advised me to try reusable organic cotton pads or a reusable cup to collect my flow. Um, no. Thank you, kind sir, but I'll decline your counsel on matters of the female monthly cycle. And for now I'll decline anything reusable. (Please note: This is one of the few times when I didn't enthusiastically embrace, or even entertain, the idea of a reusable option.)

However, that guy was onto something with the organic idea. Typical tampons are made from rayon—which is derived from wood pulp in an energy-intensive process that wastes about two-thirds of the wood material—and nonorganic cotton. The tampons are then bleached with chlorine that releases dioxins. And many feature plastic applicators. Yeah, these tampons aren't getting recycled.

But there are a few companies out there making tampons—that really work—out of organic cotton. For applicator lovers (and I don't blame you), Natracare (natracare.com) makes a certified organic cotton, non-chlorine-bleached tampon with a cardboard thing-a-ma-jig instead of plastic. Or you could take it a step further and reduce the paraphernalia with an applicator-free product. Seventh Generation (seventhgen.com) makes organic cotton, chlorine-free tampons of this ilk. I took one for the team and tried this—after swearing I'd never *not* use an applicator—and you know what? Once you get the hang of it (give it two to three insertions) you'll never miss it.

And given that you'll use about eleven thousand tampons over the course of your menstrual years, going with the organic flow (hee-hee . . . flow) makes a difference.

Tip: While you're pondering the impact of the using organic cotton versus nonorganic when cousin Rosie comes to town (that euphemism comes courtesy of my mom), think about the other cotton products you use in the pursuit of truth and beauty. Or just beauty. Like cotton swabs, balls, and rounds. Choose organic there, too. Organic Essentials (organicessentials.com) makes a line of soft and well-priced products (about $3 for a package of one hundred cotton balls).

Scent of a woman

As I perused the personal care products at Whole Foods one day, I realized that I hadn't yet ventured into the deodorant and antiperspirant section. Here's the thing: I sweat. Sometimes a lot. Especially in the middle of summer (it was August). Oh, and I can get pretty ripe, too, if I haven't showered or I forget to slap on the roll-on. I do not have a whole lot of confidence in a product that promises to keep me smelling fresh with botanicals such as sage and lemongrass. So I stalled this particular experiment till the mainstream deodorant I was using ran out. After all, living green is about consuming less, not wasting what you've already got. I milked that thing to the bitter (but sweet-smelling) end.

When I mentioned the impending switch to Will, he asked me what harm, exactly, the little bit of deodorant I was putting onto my body each morning was doing to the environment. (He's totally on board conceptually with using natural products to replace anything that goes down the drain or directly into the water supply.)

For deodorant, it's not so much where it goes once you own it, although you do shower it off down the drain and some might seep into the water if you're swimming. In this case, though, it's more about production of the product. Natural deodorants are free of aluminum, the mining of which does a number on the environment (extraction and processing uses a ton of energy and releases pollutants such as fluorine gas into the air, and transporting it—because it's generally mined far, far away from the United States—uses more energy still). Aluminum, an ingredient in conventional antiperspirants, has also been linked to breast cancer and Alzheimer's. Many antiperspirants and deodorants contain unhealthy chemicals such as parabens, propylene glycol, talc, and triclosan, the antibacterial agent that can react to become chloroform.

Anyway, when I couldn't possibly scrape another use out of my beloved Shower Fresh Mitchum, I went to the store and started sniffing potential replacements. The least vile—and let me tell you, some of these things made me recoil when I opened them— was a calendula-scented situation from Tom's of Maine. I got that and a few others (had to try a crystal deodorant stick, too). I put it on the next morning, and Will immediately told me that I smelled "like a man." Thanks, sweetie. You, too.

He was right.

And it got worse.

I was at a lunch meeting that afternoon when I noticed that someone sitting near me had a hint of b.o. Gross. Oh, wait. Nope, not someone sitting near me. Me. Great. I ran home before going to my next meeting. Okay, I walked slowly because, by the way, natural deodorants are not antiperspirants and my armpits were getting more soaked by the second—wreaking havoc, I was sure, on my cute and expensive white organic cotton tee (more about those on page 120). When I got home, I slapped on one of the other brands of natural deodorant I'd purchased. It didn't help. (This is also when I noticed that none of my chosen products came in recyclable packaging. What the hell?)

At this point I decided to cut my losses and go for a run so I had a good excuse to take a shower before the dinner I had to attend that night. I washed ferociously and layered on yet another kind of natural deodorant.

It's normally a ten-minute walk to the Four Seasons, where my dinner was being held. That night it took me sixteen minutes. I don't hang out there very often, and I did not want to stink and sweat all over the place. So I walked very, very slowly (and admittedly considered hopping in a cab, but decided to stick to my "no cars when you can easily walk" guns), kept the perspiration to a bare minimum, and managed to get through the evening without offending my dinner companions. I walked home at my normal pace, and sniffed myself when I got there. It wasn't awful, but it wasn't great. This was three hours post-shower. I'd meant to use natural deodorant for at least a week—if not permanently—but I knew then and there I just couldn't keep this up. I could not be a lifestyle writer with a rep for smelling icky.

I know it's not very green of me, but I restocked my supply of Shower Fresh Mitchum the next day. The deodorant is one thing I'm not going to do. (Critics, fire away!)

Tip: If your odor and perspiration levels are such that you can deal with using the natural stuff, that's great. Try Alba's Clear Enzyme deodorant (albabotanica.com), Dr. Hauschka Deodorant Fresh (drhauschka.com), or—if you want to go semi-green—the aluminum- and paraben-free Adidas 24-hour Control, which offers antiperspirant and deodorant assistance.

TREAT YOURSELF TO RELAXATION (GREENLY)

This is the fun part of the chapter. The part where I stop telling you about all the things you *shouldn't* use—although I prefer to think of it as encouraging you to discover fantastic, healthy, beauty-enhancing new goodies—and tell you what you *should* do. Usually I don't love the word "should"—it suggests some screwed up imperative to confirm to societal standards. Or something like that.

But here's one thing that's a big, giant should: You should chill out and pamper yourself. As often as possible. This is what a psychotherapist I know refers to as "self-care," and it's, like, wicked good for your mental health. It can also help you look stunning: Stress has been proven to cause breakouts, speed the aging process, make skin look sallow, and promote weight gain. So relax!

Get massages. Get reflexology. Get facials. Make appointments at spas that use products you'd use at home (you know, truly all-natural and chemical-free). If you aren't sure where to look, pick up a copy of *Organic Spa* magazine. Yes, there's a whole magazine about this. And these spas are all over the place.

If regular spa treatments don't fit in the budget, get your s.o. to give you a good back or foot rub, and return the favor. Give yourself a pedi (sans polish and with healthy scrubs and moisturizers from Kiss My Face (kissmyface.com), Red Flower (redflower.com), or the Rhode Island-based organic skincare line Farmaesthetics (farmaesthetics.com)). I pick one day a week (it's Thursday, if you were wondering), and I promise myself that I will pamper myself in some way, even some small way, every time it rolls around. Even if I think I don't have time, I do it. G-Spa, a fabulous quickie spa on Newbury Street in Boston that uses Farmaesthetics products, offers a fifteen-minute neck and shoulder massage for fifteen bucks. It gets the kinks out fast.

Do. Not. Smoke. Ever.

Let's forget about the environmental implications for a moment. Actually, let's not. Growing tobacco uses crazy amounts of pesticides. It's the sixth most pesticide-ridden crop in the United States, using more than 25 million pounds each year. The smoke from cigarettes is ten times more polluting than exhaust from diesel fuel. Worldwide, smoking emits more than 5.5 billion pounds of CO_2 and more than 11 billion pounds of methane annually. Considering that methane is twenty-three times more potent as a greenhouse gas than CO_2, that's the equivalent of about 235 pounds of CO_2 per smoker per year. Then there's all the packaging, and the fact that so many smokers use the sidewalk as an ashtray.

There are, of course, myriad health woes associated with smoking. But you've heard all those, and you know they're true, and this chapter's about getting gorgeous. Ms. Lovely, smoking does not make you gorgeous. It thins the skin and leads to premature wrinkling and discoloration. It stains your teeth. It gives you bad breath. It makes your hair—now so nicely scented with citrusy essential oils—smell awful. I don't care if you're out one night and your friends are smoking. Please, please, please don't light up. Thank you.

CALL IT A NIGHT

Without question, the very best thing you can do to bring out your natural beauty has zero negative impact on the environment: **Get plenty of sleep.** As often as you can. Preferably every night. (Maybe in some organic sheets?)

It's called beauty sleep for a reason. Studies show getting enough sleep helps your skin look better and prevents weight gain. This is when your cells repair themselves—give them the time they need. Anecdotal evidence: I got mono about two years ago (no, I did not catch it from kissing a sixteen-year-old boy) and for a month I slept more than I'd slept in years. My skin looked great. I know it's unscientific, but I'm convinced it was all the sleep.

Why is this green, you ask? If your skin looks better naturally, maybe you won't need as many products as you thought you did. You never know.

Go to bed. You can read more in the morning. Good night.

Chapter Six

GREEN IS THE NEW BLACK

I recently read an article that advised readers to stop buying things if they wanted to lessen their negative impact on the environment. Seriously, that was the advice. Stop shopping for everything except absolute essentials like food and toilet paper, and make do with what you already have. Um . . . yeah, *right*. True, consuming just about anything is eco-detrimental (production, packaging, and shipping all take their toll) but that doesn't mean I'm going to wear last year's designer denim for the next eight seasons. Please.

Here's a more realistic plan: Be thoughtful about the clothes and accessories you buy and the habits you use when buying and taking care of them. (This chapter's got tips on how to do that.) Along with the process of lightening your environmental footprint, there's a surprising added bonus—you'll probably cut way down on buyer's remorse. My "why the hell is that in my closet?" purchases are close to zero since I've started being an eco-conscious shopper. I get more compliments and "*where* did you find that?" questions from my friends, including my fashion editor friends.

Keep in mind that this chapter is *not* about getting rid of all the "non-green" clothing you own and buying an entirely new ecofriendly wardrobe. That wouldn't be green at all. But when you do get a craving for something fabulous, here are a bunch of ideas to help you become a greener fashionista. Because though going green should never be just a fashion statement, green really is the new black.

EDIT YOUR CLOSET

One of the first things a personal shopper or personal stylist—you have both of those, right?—will do for you is go through your closet and pare it down so it only contains things you love, love, love to wear. (I know this not because I have a staff of stylists and shoppers, but because I've interviewed them for fashion stories and paid attention, so I could use their advice and not have to pay for it. There are definitely perks to my job sometimes. Anyway.)

The idea is that if you love *everything* in your closet—even if you end up with a third of the clothes you had before you started the editing process—you'll have a much easier time getting dressed in the morning and you'll always look (and believe that you look) stunning.

This is definitely a less-is-more situation. Crap in your closet—pieces that don't fit, don't flatter, or make you feel like you're wearing a tent—distracts from the amazing stuff that's already in there. And if you're distracted from the amazing stuff that's already in there, you might think you need to go on a shopping spree to save you from wardrobe hatred. This is not a green solution. Edit first, 'kay?

To get started, go through *every single item* in your closet. If you hate it and you know it, put it into the NO pile. (At the end, please donate said NO pile to a women's shelter, bring it to a clothing swap, or consign it. Do not toss it into the trash so it makes its way to a landfill. Thank you.) If you love it and you know it, put it into a YES pile. I do not believe in a MAYBE pile—you know you're just going to keep it, and then what's the point? If you're not sure about a piece, try it on and assess how it looks, how it makes you feel, and what you can wear it with. If you look smokin,' and you can think of an upcoming situation where you'll want to wear it, and you have stuff that looks good with it, it's a yes. If you don't like how it looks, or you know, realistically, that you just won't wear it, it's a no. Don't cry. Let it go. You don't love it, and it certainly doesn't love you back.

If something you love is in a state of disrepair, assess whether it can be fixed. If so, *get it fixed* instead of buying a new one. If not, say goodbye. And learn from the experience: Take care of the clothing you love, and be fastidious about getting it straightened up at the first sign of an unraveling thread, missing button, or wee little hole.

Finally, don't stop editing. Go in early (before malaise sets in) and often, and weed out anything not stupendous. And the next time you shop (and forever thereafter), don't buy *anything* you think might wind up in a NO pile. It will only get in the way of your relationship with the clothes you love. (The ones in which you are *so* chic. Admit it.)

BAG BAGS, COMPLETELY 🖋

Remember those *Sex and the City* scenes where Carrie Bradshaw would come breezing through her door and drop an armload of Manolo Blahnik and Barneys bags? I'm not going to suggest you give up shopping sprees altogether, but it's a good idea to avoid that kind of bag orgy. Shopping bags—both paper and plastic—are bigger environmental offenders than you might realize. I mentioned this briefly on page 19 in the Little Green Things chapter, where I suggested popping little purchases into your purse. But I think you're ready to take it to the next level. Are you with me? We should bang knuckles or something right now. Instead I'll explain why.

Let's start with plastic: According to the Environmental Protection Agency (EPA), close to a trillion plastic bags are used worldwide each year. The United States used about one hundred billion of those. That's—yikes—almost one thousand plastic bags per year per U.S. household—meaning even one household opting out of plastic bags makes a noticeable dent. It takes twelve million barrels of oil to produce the plastic bags the United States alone uses each year. Fewer than 3 percent of plastic bags are recycled—meaning they end up in landfills (where they can take hundreds of years to degrade) and often in streams, rivers, and oceans, where they choke and poison about one hundred thousand whales, birds, and turtles each year and act as rafts to carry foreign species to places where they can do damage to existing ecosystems. What's more, most plastic bags are made from polyethylene, which is derived from petroleum or natural gas (you know by now those are nonrenewable resources). When they do break down—and they don't safely or completely biodegrade—they release toxic chemicals into the earth's air, soil, and water.

And then there's paper: I used to think these were better for the environment than plastic because they are biodegradable. Nope. Making ten billion paper bags (about the number of grocery bags Americans use in a year) requires fourteen million trees to be cut down. And then manufacturing them, which involves heating wood chips in a chemical solution at high temperature, takes four times more energy than manufacturing plastic bags, and produces 70 percent more air pollutants and 50 percent more water pollutants. Only 20 percent of paper bags are recycled, and they take up nine times as much space in landfills as plastic bags do.

If everyone in New York City alone used *just one* less shopping bag per year, it would eliminate 5 million pounds of waste (counting the bags themselves, the tree waste, and the stuff that goes into making them) and save the city $250,000 in disposal costs. As we discussed on page 19, bags that are a hybrid of paper and plastic (like so many fancy laminated shopping bags are) are the worst, because they are rarely recyclable.

The solution? Don't use shopping bags at all.

This is an easy green shopping strategy to employ. Every single time you head out to go shopping (whether you're just browsing or picking up a bottle of wine and a wedge of cheese or going for a serious wardrobe or home overhaul), be prepared with a sturdy, reusable bag. I'm a huge fan of the L.L. Bean Boat & Tote bags, and I have them in every size (and several colors). If uber-elegant is the only thing that works for you, consider this the perfect excuse to invest in that beautiful bag you've been coveting. You'd be doing it to save the earth! Keep it right by your door and use it exclusively for shopping, so it's always clean, empty, and waiting for you.

Tip: Let the salesperson know—nicely!—as soon as you get to the register that you don't need a bag. That way they won't beat you to the punch and start swaddling your purchase in tissue paper and ribbon while you're looking down to hunt for your credit card.

Expect resistance. The frequency with which my "I don't need a bag, thanks" gets met with looks of mild scorn surprises me, but for whatever reason shopkeepers—especially those in trendy boutiques and department stores—don't like to send you away *sans* sack. When I bought a cute little tote from Marc Jacobs—*the proceeds from which were going to fight global warming*—I practically had to beg the salesperson not to wrap it in wads of tissue and stuff it in another bag. If you're prepared for people to challenge you on this, it's a little easier to stand your ground with a smile.

OPT FOR ORGANIC COTTON

It's easy to assume that all natural fibers, including cotton, are ecofriendly. That's what I used to think, and I was probably even kind of snooty about it. Turns out I was off the mark. Some natural fibers are fantastic, but conventionally grown cotton is not. It's actually an environmental disaster.

Here's why: As I mentioned in the section about organic cotton sheets on page 51, growing conventional cotton is *the* most pesticide-intensive farming process in the world. Only about 3 percent of the world's farmland is used for growing cotton, yet conventional cotton growth uses about 24 percent of all the insecticides in the world as well as 11 percent of all pesticides—which permeate the air, damage the soil, and seep into the water supply. Every pound of cotton (which is about how much it takes to make one T-shirt) is sprayed with a third of a pound of pesticides—and a total of 50 million pounds of pesticides are used on cotton in the United States alone. Then there are the chemical fertilizers—more than 2 billion pounds (142 pounds per acre) are used annually to grow conventional cotton in the United States.

By the way, all those pesticides and fertilizers in the cotton fields translate to about a third of a cup of chemicals (which include such known cancer-causing agents as cyanide, dicofol, naled, propargite, and trifluralin) remaining in your cute little cotton tee. Which you're probably wearing right next to your skin.

Organic cotton is grown without any pesticides or chemical fertilizers, meaning none of that seeps into the air, the water, the soil, or your skin. The organic cotton industry is growing rapidly (the women's apparel segment of it is growing the fastest, at about 35 percent per year) and it's getting easier and easier to find organic cotton in the form of luxe goods such as silky soft tees. Plus, it's appearing in totally affordable products such as American Apparel (americanapparel.com) tees (around $15) and sexy little thongs ($8), Wal-Mart pajamas (about $12), and Danskin yoga pants ($14-ish).

Shopping for organic cotton at Wal-Mart doesn't excite you? Okay, you can also find it from such fashion-forward designers as Loomstate (organic jeans designed by Rogan Gregory; loomstate.org), Edun (the cutting-edge label founded by Bono's wife, Ali Hewson; edun.ie), Linda Loudermilk (some Hollywood celebs wore her to the Oscars; lindaloudermilk.com), and my personal favorite, Stewart+Brown (a California-based line featuring perfectly cut, expensive-but-worth-it tees, skirts, and sweaters; stewartbrown.com). More designer denim options include the incredibly flattering jeans from Del Forte (delforte.com) and the new organic denim line from everybody's favorite maker of jeans, Levi's (levi.com).

Tip: Try it out! For a short period of time, like two months, commit to buying only organic if you're picking up any item of cotton clothing (jeans, tees, underwear). You'll probably find yourself wasting less money on cheap trendy items that you'll never wear—and you'll love the way the fabric feels next to your body. And you may get other benefits: Will tends to give me more spontaneous backrubs when I'm wearing an organic cotton tee. Then there are the compliments—I was wearing a Stewart+Brown organic cotton skirt at dinner the other night and my friend Kate couldn't stop touching it. Of course she asked where I got it because it was so soft and such a great skirt, and she wanted one. I found it at Envi (shopenvi.com), a new eco-boutique on Newbury Street in

Boston that has a great online shop as well. (Stewart+Brown is also sold at boutiques all over the country—check stewartbrown.com to find a retail location near you.) Anyway, chances are you'll be a total convert after your self-imposed only-organic restricted period, but if not, you can always go back to conventional for some of your purchases—just try to buy organic whenever it's convenient.

Shopping strategy: Is there a boutique near you that carries chic organic cotton pieces? Let them know you love it, and tell your friends to support their efforts, too.

Tip: Just because a cotton item is a natural color doesn't mean it's organic. I know you already figured that out, but I just read an article about "green" fashion in a certain high-end lifestyle magazine, and the page was filled with clothes in shades of cream, tan, and taupe—but not even half of them were organic. Read the label. If it's organic, it will say so.

BE A MATERIAL GIRL

In terms of natural fibers, cotton is decidedly the worst environmental offender. So if you only pick one to think about, that should be it. If you want to take it further, here's the scoop on some other great fabrics.

Wool: Wool is, theoretically, a renewable resource. It's shorn from sheep, and it grows back to be shorn again the next year. And it can be grown sustainably, if the sheep are allowed to free-graze.

However, most conventionally farmed sheep are now kept in too-small areas and sprayed with chemicals to keep mice and lice away (in total, sheep get treated with about 14,000 pounds of pesticides per year in the United States—much less pesticide than is used for cotton, but still too much) and many are given feed that contains antibiotics, which can ultimately contaminate groundwater, so they'll grow faster. Conventional manufacturing of wool generally involves bleaching, formaldehyde application, and chemical dyes. The worst woolen culprits are new "technological" wools that claim to resist shrinking—those are definitely treated extensively with chemicals such as chlorine. If possible, skip the "smart" wool, and look for organically grown and manufactured wool. If you can't find that, at least try to find wools that haven't been chemically treated and dyed. Look for non-dyed wool in gorgeous natural colors, or wool that's been dyed with dirt or clay dyes or ecofriendly fiber-reactive dyes. Alpaca wool, which is naturally softer and stronger than sheep wool and even when conventionally produced uses less chemical treatment, is a particularly ecofriendly wool choice. John Patrick Organic (johnpatrickorganic.com) and Indigenous Designs (indigenousdesigns.com) have sweaters you'll want to sleep in. I mean, you'll want to wear them in public, too, but you won't want to take them off. I have an ivory sweater coat from John Patrick Organic that I wore five days in a row one week.

Cashmere: This might sound like an overstatement, but I couldn't live without cashmere. (Okay, it's an overstatement. Barely.) Really, though, if living green required giving up cashmere I'd have to think long and hard about that one. Luckily, it doesn't. Whew. In fact, high-quality cashmere is one of the most sustainable fibers around. It's combed from the underhairs of cashmere (or Kashmir) goats, which are native to the Himalayas but are now raised on farms in many parts of the world. As with regular wool, though, cashmere (especially lower quality) is often chemically treated and dyed and blended with other fibers. Yes, even things labeled 100 percent cashmere, if they aren't great quality. So get the good stuff, and learn where your cashmere comes from and what's been done to it before you snuggle up. In case you were wondering, Stewart+Brown, my favorite organic cotton T-shirt maker, also has a line of stunning ecofriendly cashmere. Deborah Lindquist (deborahlindquist.com) makes her sustainable cashmere pieces edgy—don't expect prim pastel twinsets here.

Linen: I think linen is one of the most elegant fabrics ever. Crisp, cool, and a little bit wrinkly, it looks perfect in a summer sundress or a guy's shirt (especially when it's untucked and the guy is barefoot on the beach . . .). It's made from the flax plant, which even when not grown organically requires little in the way of pesticides and chemicals. Still, organic is even better . . . and you should look for linen in natural shades that haven't been bleached, extensively treated, or chemically dyed. (Which is a good choice anyway: That gorgeous summer linen dress just wouldn't look right in harsh lime green.) As with cashmere, look for high-quality, 100 percent linen that hasn't been blended with synthetics or nonorganic cotton. Brooklyn-based designer Caitlin Mociun (mociun.com) uses linen in dresses that will definitely make people stop and ask where you got it. Shop for Mociun and other linen pieces at Beklina (beklina.com).

Silk: Being ecofriendly gets easier and easier when you realize that some of the most luxurious fashion fabrics are some of the most sustainable. Count silk among those renewable and biodegradable fabrics, especially high quality (preferably organic) silk that hasn't been chemically treated or blended with synthetics. Coolnotcruel (coolnotcruel.com) is a New York City designer making slinky, silk slip dresses as well as alpaca sweaters and great pants, skirts, and tops.

Tip: Find eco-fashions from organic cotton, undyed wool, alpaca, cashmere, silk, and linen online at Green With Glamour (greenwithglamour.com), The Green Loop (thegreen-loop.com), and Pangaya (pangaya.com).

Shopping strategy: Always go for quality, not quantity. My mom used to tell me that it's better to have one beautiful, high-quality, amazing sweater than four cheap ones. And she was right. If you build your wardrobe from a few classic, stunning, well-made pieces that you adore instead of tons of trendy throwaway clothes, you'll look better (cheap looks cheap, and that's that), your clothes will last longer (meaning you won't need to buy so much stuff—and you'll probably end up saving money because you aren't spending it every other day on an inexpensive item you'll only wear once), and getting dressed every day will be a much more satisfying and pleasurable experience.

WATCH YOUR WORKOUT GEAR

Generally speaking, I don't like wearing clothes made from synthetic materials. Acrylic sweater, anyone? No, thank you. The exception is when I'm working out. Old cotton T-shirts just don't wick sweat away like technologically advanced fabrics do, and they don't tend to be particularly body-conscious (i.e., they don't look that good and they can get in your way). Because I tend to glow profusely (who am I kidding? I am a sweat-ball after a run or a bike ride) and get klutzy when I'm tired, I'm ever so much more comfortable in gear made expressly for exercise purposes.

Problem is, most workout gear is made from non-earth-friendly synthetic fabrics such as nylon and polyester. These materials are manufactured from petrochemicals, the creation of which releases nitrous oxide into the environment. This is bad stuff. Nitrous oxide is a greenhouse gas that's 310 times stronger (hence, 310 times worse for the environment) than carbon dioxide. And it's not just a little nitrous oxide that's coming from the conventional production of these fabrics. The production of nylon, for example, accounts for 90 percent of the use of the world's adipic acid. Adipic acid, according to the Environmental Protection Agency, is the largest potential source of industrial nitrous oxide emissions.

Good news: You can find plenty of fabulous, form-fitting, functional workout apparel made from ecofriendly fabrics. Be Present (bepresent.com) offers stretchy tops and pants made from bamboo, one of the world's most renewable materials. Patagonia (patagonia.com) sells capilene base layers made from recycled polyester. (If you're going to buy polyester, recycled is the way to go—it uses 76 percent less energy and results in a 71 percent reduction of carbon dioxide emissions compared to making polyester from new raw materials.) Prana (prana.com) makes extremely sexy tops and bottoms from organic cotton and other natural materials and recycled synthetics. You should also look for workout gear made from hemp—I know it's a cliché to recommend hemp, but it *is* ecofriendly and, more importantly, nice and breathable—as well as lyocell (a synthetic fiber made from plant cellulose), which often goes by the brand name Tencel, and even wool, a tried-and-true hiking staple that has kept moisture away from the skin for thousands of years.

Hold the PVC, please

In the world of conventional workout gear, PVC (polyvinyl chloride—sometimes just called vinyl—I've already trashed vinyl a few times in this book, especially on pages 42 and 46) is everywhere. But that's changing, and it will change even faster if fashionable fitness types demand and buy products without PVC. Why should you go PVC-free? The manufacturing of this plastic releases dioxins into the environment, and dioxins are a potent carcinogenic that, according to the World Health Organization, are one of "a special group of dangerous chemicals known as persistent organic pollutants. Once dioxins have entered the environment or body, they are there to stay due to their uncanny ability to dissolve in fats and to their rock-solid chemical stability." Asics (asics.com) and New Balance (newbalance.com) make running shoes sans PVC, and Jade Yoga (jadeyoga.com) produces an outstanding line of PVC-free Harmony yoga mats. I use one of those in San Francisco, and I have the Eco mat from Lululemon (lululemon.com) in Boston.

Tip: Don't just toss your old running shoes into the garbage so they wind up in some landfill. Either donate them to an organization such as One World Running (oneworldrunning.org) that distributes running shoes to those who couldn't otherwise afford them or, if they're in sorry shape, give them to a program such as Nike Reuse-A-Shoe (nike.com), which recycles all the materials from old shoes and turns them into athletic surfaces like soccer and football fields, basketball and tennis courts, tracks, and playground surfacing for kids.

Catalog faults

Sometimes that perfect pair of high boots or those magically flattering pants are only available via mail order. If that's the case, go online to make your purchase—do not shop from paper catalogs. Instead, call the toll-free number of any company that sends you a catalog—seventeen billion of them are mailed in the United States each year, meaning the average household gets more than 150 catalogs annually; only about 7 percent are printed on even partially recycled paper—and ask to be removed from their mailing list. If you need to know when the new fall line is available, add yourself to the e-mail list instead.

CONSIDER VINTAGE 🖋

This is not where I tell you to find all your clothes in thrift stores because of all the hidden treasures potentially lurking amid the crap. I suppose it's true that you could find a gem in any thrift store. And if you're one of the charmed few who *always* unearths something fabulous from consignment shops— great. Lucky you. I am not one of those people. Some thrift stores, quite frankly, skeeve me out.

But if you need a specific item—say, a unique party dress or an elegant suit—that you simply can't find from an eco-conscious designer in an ecofriendly fabric, seeking a vintage version is a wonderfully eco-conscious alternative. Why? Because a piece of clothing that was crafted long ago costs nothing to the environment today. No pesticides sprayed to grow fibers for new fabric. No energy used or chemicals released in the making of a new synthetic material. No material or chemical waste. No plastic, cardboard, or other new packaging—and quite possibly no energy used in shipping. Beyond all that, industrial manufacturing of new garments usually involves treating fabrics with chlorine bleach and other volatile organic compounds, the by-products of which are released into the air and water supply. With vintage clothing, that's not a problem. What's more, the U.S. Customs and Border Protection Agency requires that the packing materials for *any* garment or fabric made overseas be either heat-treated to a core temperature of over 130 degrees for thirty minutes or sprayed with methyl bromide, a Class 1 ozone-depleting substance (fifty times stronger than CFCs) that's toxic and potentially deadly to humans. Because the heat treatment is time-consuming (not to mention expensive in terms of energy expenditure), methyl bromide is the prevailing procedure. Again, don't need to worry about that with vintage.

Who knew buying a gorgeous forty-year-old Chanel suit is actually a way to preserve the planet? Sign me up. The thing is, though, you'll only stick with vintage if finding it isn't a miserable experience. Don't comb through awful secondhand shops hoping for a miracle—you won't find what you're looking for there, anyway. Go to *nice* vintage and consignment shops. Start looking locally for sure, because if you buy something from afar, it's going to have to be shipped. Shipping requires energy (transportation) and packaging (a whole lot of wasted paper and plastic) and if you can avoid that, you should. DailyCandy (dailycandy.com) offers twelve different city editions, plus an "Everywhere" edition, that may be able to point you to high-end vintage clothing or consignment shops near you.

If there isn't a good vintage shop or high-end consignment boutique near you, go online. eBay (ebay.com) is a shockingly good source of amazing vintage fashion. On a recent visit I found a mint condition Burberry peacoat (for $22), a perfect Schiaparelli cardigan (for $289), and a stunning black cocktail dress from—yes—Chanel (for $450). More concentrated selections of couture can be found at Fashion Dig (fashiondig.com), a site dripping in Gucci and Pucci and Dior (oh my!), and DecadesTwo (decadestwo.com), a Los Angeles-based, insanely swanky (ciao, Balenciaga and Valentino) consignment and vintage shop that offers online shopping. For a New York City take, try Chelsea Girl (chelsea-girl.com). When it comes to finding knockout signature pieces for prices that won't knock out your entire savings, once you go vintage you may never go back.

You can also shop for "new" lines by designers who do the vintage digging for you. Celeb fave Deborah Lindquist (deborahlindquist.com) reconstructs vintage clothing and accessories into drop-dead one-of-a-kind pieces. Her bustiers, corsets, and dresses are some of the most wearably sexy things you'll ever see. Libertine culls beautifully tailored vintage suits and blouses and adds a fray here and a silkscreen there, and the result is a rocker-slash-conservative chic that no one has been able to duplicate. Ask the owners of your favorite local boutique if they carry anything made from vintage materials. You may be surprised at the fabulous stuff they show you.

Swapping strategy: Would you rather get "vintage" clothes from people you know than from strangers? I hear you. Next time you have your girlfriends over for wine, have a clothing swap. Everyone shows up with a minimum number of gently worn (or never-worn and never-returned) items that they don't want anymore, you lay them out, and take your pick. Donate anything that isn't selected to a local women's shelter. Visit clothingswap.org for ideas.

Tip: When you're sick of something in your closet, do not just throw it away. In the United States we throw away about 35 pounds of used textiles each per year, for a total of almost 9 billion pounds. That makes up almost 5 percent of municipal waste. If it's a total mess, cut it up and use it as cleaning rags or drop it off at a recycling facility that accepts textiles. If it's in decent shape, give it to a friend or your younger sister, or donate it to a local shelter or a disaster relief effort.

Support the Locals

"Eat local" is green foodie slogan, and "shop local" should be a mantra of green fashionistas. Mass-producing, packaging, and shipping something thousands of miles is extremely costly to the environment, whether the something in question is potato chips, lettuce (it takes 4,600 calories of fossil fuel energy to get one package of lettuce across the country . . . and clothes are way heavier than lettuce), or pleated khakis (not that you're wearing pleated khakis). If you have to choose between buying clothes from a giant chain store that mass-produces its stores in factories far, far, far overseas or a local independent designer, choose the local designer—preferably one working with ecofriendly or vintage fabrics. And of course, if you have a choice between walking to a small local boutique and driving to the mall, always walk to the little shop. While you're in, talk to the owners, get to know them, and ask them to carry more ecofriendly fashions.

GET GREEN BLING

I hate to be the one to tell you this, but diamonds are not a green girl's best friend. And all that's gold is *not* green. Sorry.

Unfortunately, obtaining the natural elements—diamonds, other gemstones, gold, platinum—that go into traditional beautiful jewelry is not an environmentally beautiful practice. Accessing such materials requires mining, which consumes huge amounts of energy, releases pollutants and greenhouse gases into the air, allows toxic chemicals to seep into groundwater, damages land and speeds up erosion, and generates an unbelievable amount of waste. The use of chemicals such as cyanide and mercury to separate gold from rock is a terrible health hazard for miners who are breathing it in as well as being an environmental hazard.

Mining is also associated with many socially devastating practices, especially in African countries such as Angola and Sierra Leone, where the diamond industry has been known to fund violence against innocent civilians. The United Nations calls these conflict diamonds, and they define them as "diamonds that originate from areas controlled by forces or factions opposed to legitimate and internationally recognized governments, and are used to fund military action in opposition to those governments, or in contravention of the decisions of the Security Council." This is too huge a topic to address in great detail here—but if you're going to buy a new diamond, make sure it comes with a certificate of origin, and is certified conflict-free. Keep reading to find out where to buy.

Mining is not a small industry. In the United States, mining consumes about 5 percent of the total electricity the country uses. In countries such as South Africa, where there's a richer concentration of "valuable" materials, the consumption is much higher—around 25 percent of total energy consumption. Not all this mining is for jewelry—but a surprisingly large amount of it is: Of the 2,500 tons of gold that are mined each year, for example, 80 percent of it goes into jewelry. And according to Oxfam America, the production of one little 18-karat ring that weighs less than an ounce creates more than 20 tons of mine waste. One ring.

Fear not: This doesn't mean you have to stop getting jewelry as a gift (or treating yourself to that perfect bauble to celebrate . . . whatever). There are eco-chic jewelers out there making gorgeous pieces—not the clunky beaded stuff you might imagine green types have to wear. There are sparkly rings, sleek bracelets, and shiny earrings made from recycled gold and platinum and "created" diamonds and gemstones—synthetic stones that match the quality of the natural kind are now available from high-end companies such as Apollo (apollodiamond.com). Trust me (the gal who doesn't particularly like synthetics): They can be gorgeous.

GreenKarat (greenkarat.com) uses synthetic diamonds and gems as well as recycled gold and platinum in everything from minimalist diamond-studded wedding bands to eye-popping triple stone rings. Brilliant Earth (brilliantearth.com) offers engagement rings and wedding bands made from recycled metals and conflict-free diamonds (these are my personal favorites); Leber Jeweler (leberjeweler.com) has an Earthwise line of classic diamond studs, engagement rings, and gemstone pendants made of reclaimed metals and conflict-free stones. And—ready for some happy news?—Tiffany (tiffany.com) is making great strides toward ecofriendliness. Their diamonds are certified conflict-free (and their efforts in promoting this have led to more stringent oversight of the diamond industry in general), they mine metals responsibly, they are part of the No Dirty Gold campaign, and they don't use coral because its harvesting can damage marine habitats. Oh, and those little blue boxes are made from Forest Stewardship Council-certified paper.

Another alternative—one that demands an even smaller ecological price than even ecofriendly new gems—is to choose antique jewelry. Made from metals and stones mined decades (or centuries) ago, it's an extremely low-impact choice and a great way to find pieces that won't look like something everyone (or anyone) you know is wearing. Or you could take a stone that your mother or grandmother had (hey, it'll have even more meaning) and have your jeweler set it into a ring or pendant for you. But now you need to find a jeweler that's willing to use (and knows how to get) recycled metals, huh? Contact Ethical Metalsmiths (ethicalmetalsmiths.org) to find a jeweler near you. Or recycle your old jewelry. If there's a piece you don't wear anymore, have a jeweler melt it down and create something you actually want to wear.

Just say yes

Insisting on green bling might be a little high-maintenance, but it can also encourage creativity in the givers of the bling. When Will and I got engaged (which happened just as I was finishing this book), he knew I would want an ecofriendly or vintage ring. But he had no idea where to find it, so—get this—he carved me a temporary ring out of (reclaimed) wood. No, he's not the jewelry-making type, so this was très unexpected, and I couldn't have loved it more. Then we picked out a beautiful ring—a simple band of tiny conflict-free diamonds and responsibly mined platinum—together. I know, I know, hard-core environmentalists would say the more responsible choice would be to forego the ring. What can I say? I don't wear much jewelry, but sometimes a girl wants a ring. And this is one I plan to wear forever.

Tip: Institute a "waiting period," not just for jewelry, but for any purchase. This is good eco-shopping advice, but it's also just plain good shopping advice. If there's even a hint of doubt in your mind—and maybe even if you think there's no hint of doubt in your mind but the item you're totally craving is expensive or, okay, isn't particularly ecofriendly—walk away for an hour or, better, a day. Put it on hold if you think someone else will snap it up. Sleep on it. There's a decent chance you'll realize you don't really need it. And if you *do* still want it, it's probably something that you really love, something that belongs in your closet. Having a waiting period helps you weed out what you don't really need, and makes you a more conscious consumer all around.

A woman's right to Choos

I've tried to convert to ecofriendly footwear—that is, shoes that are entirely leather and PVC-free and manufactured in an earth-conscious way. I really have. And I admire those who can do it. Stella McCartney (stellamccartney.com) is making it a lot easier with her sweet line of shoes. And the shoes from Charmone (charmone.com), also leather-free, PVC-free, and packaged in recycled boxes, are my new favorites. But here's the thing: Occasionally I have a weakness for Jimmy Choo shoes. (Oops.) Sometimes just looking at a pair of them makes me catch my breath because they are so beautiful. I realize they're just shoes. Whatever. I definitely can't afford an entire Choo shoe wardrobe, but I've scored a few pairs on sale and even paid full retail once or twice. I just didn't pay my electric bill those months. (Kidding. Now that I use CFLs, my electric bill is way cheap.) The point is, because I have a Choo or two doesn't mean I can't go green in many or most other areas of my life. We all slip up every now and then. That's okay. Don't give up the green.

USE A GREENER DRY CLEANER 🍃

So in an ideal world, you have a closet filled only with clothes and accessories you love, and you'll be making environmentally thoughtful fashion choices whenever (or *almost* whenever) you buy something new. Nice. Now you've got to keep all those sumptuous cashmere sweaters and sexy silk tops in good shape. Easy, right? Just suck up the expense—have you ever walked out of your local dry cleaner feeling like you've just been robbed?—and pay for them to be dry-cleaned on a regular basis. Actually, that's the worst thing you could do—for your clothes and for the environment.

Standard dry cleaning involves submerging clothing in petroleum-based liquid chemicals (it's called "dry" cleaning because no water is used). Somewhere between 85 percent and

95 percent of U.S. dry cleaners use a chemical called perchloroethylene, or PERC, a chlorinated hydrocarbon. It's the stuff that gives dry-cleaned items that distinctive and not-so-pleasant odor. Beyond its bad smell, if PERC is exposed to high temperatures, it breaks down into hydrogen chloride (which can cause dermatitis and other skin problems) and phosgene gas (which was used as a chemical weapon during World War I).

At normal temperatures, PERC is a skin irritant that can cause blistering, and according to the Occupational Safety & Health Administration, breathing in fumes from PERC can lead to nausea, headaches, dizziness, drowsiness, and liver and kidney damage. According to the National Cancer Institute, PERC is a possible carcinogen, and according to the EPA, PERC is a hazardous pollutant with the potential to do damage to the atmosphere, water, and soil. Older dry cleaning shops without systems in place to keep PERC from being vented directly into the air outside and leaking into the groundwater are the biggest environmental offenders, but even newer shops release tons of hazardous environmental waste. The EPA estimates that about 44,000 tons of PERC are released into the environment each year.

Of course, not all the PERC escapes into the environment. Much of it stays on your clothes, and the rest slowly evaporates into the air in your home. If you leave the plastic dry cleaning bags on your clothes, less of it will get into your air—instead, it will stay trapped on your favorite suit or cute top and start to do damage to the garment. I know someone who's a "private shopper and closet makeover consultant" (really) and she—

caring more about clothes than air quality—insists that her clients remove the bags immediately so the fantastic items she's advised them to buy don't get ruined. Oh, and speaking of those plastic bags . . . *every single piece of clothing* you bring to the dry cleaner will probably get its own bag. And plastic bags aren't so great for the environment, as you may recall from the first section of this chapter. Bottom line? Regular dry cleaning is a big don't.

This doesn't mean you need to let your delicates and other purportedly dry-clean-only items get nasty. If you want to leave it to the pros, look for ecofriendly cleaners that use either (1) wet cleaning with water and biodegradable soap—don't worry, they have systems in place to ensure fabrics don't change shape or get damaged or, (2) environmentally sound silicone solvents, which are chemically inert and safe for clothes. GreenEarth (greenearthcleaning.com) is the leader in this area, and you can find GreenEarth affiliates all over the country. When I was working on this chapter, I stopped Will on his way out the door with a load of dry cleaning and asked him to try an ecofriendly cleaner—but didn't have a good one to suggest. He was a good sport: A few minutes of online research and a phone call, and he found a green cleaner a block away. If you do choose an ecofriendly cleaner, request no plastic bags on your clothes. (Ask more than once. They don't always listen, but it's worth a shot.)

For many items, washing by hand at home is another good option. Spot test before you plunge the whole thing into water and soap or detergent (use the biodegradable kind—see more about that on page 35). (If you notice any discoloration, you may be out of luck.) I love cleaning my cashmere sweaters this way because it leaves them smelling *so* good: I use just a little ecofriendly baby shampoo (my friend Kerri recommended this to me years ago and it works beautifully) such as VedaBaby (vedababy.com) or Erbaviva (erbaviva.com) and wash my sweaters gently in lukewarm water. I don't twist them or wring them out—I just roll them gently in a towel to get the excess water out then lay them flat on a towel to dry. It takes a few minutes, yes, but it saves the hassle of trying to remember to get to the cleaners before they close . . . which is almost always about two minutes before I show up.

And dry greener, too

For clothes that don't need special treatment, you're probably just tossing them in the washer and dryer. Hopefully you're washing in cold water more often (page 24). When they come out of the wash, either line dry them completely or only use the dryer briefly to get some of the moisture and wrinkles out, then air dry them the rest of the way.

Clothes dryers are one of the bigger users of household energy—they emit an average of almost 1,500 pounds of CO_2 annually. Slash your drying time by half—and, magically, you emit 750 pounds less CO_2. Convert completely to line (or rack) drying, and you zap a major piece of your home's emissions.

If you do run the dryer, clean the lint filter every single time. That can decrease the energy used per load up to 30 percent. If you're using your own washer and dryer, no-brainer. I do not have the luxury of owning my own washer and dryer—I share it with the other peeps in my building. I have lovely neighbors, but I have a thing about touching other people's refuse, even if it is in the form of dryer lint. And if there's a hair in there, I don't even want to think about it. Other people's stray hairs are the worst—well, not the worst but one of the worst—forms of refuse. If you agree with me on this, I have no good advice for you. It's still a good idea to clean the lint tray. Just suck it up. That's what I do.

Tip: Nice rack. Find an ecofriendly drying rack, made mostly from salvaged wood, at abundantearth.com.

Chic bonus: When I lay out partially dried clothes to dry overnight in my apartment, the next morning the apartment smells like fresh laundry. That's one of my favorite smells. Especially when I use the ecofriendly Fresh Air detergent from Method (methodhome.com).

Another chic bonus: Air-drying is an easy way to get rid of static cling.

Chapter Seven

GETTING AROUND

There's nothing inherently chic about commuting or running errands, but even the chicest of people do these things every day. And the decisions you make about your daily mode(s) of transport have a big impact on your ecological footprint. The cars we drive are the source of 20 to 25 percent of all U.S. CO_2 emissions. There are a lot of things we could do to reduce those emissions—and reducing car emissions is the most important single step most individuals can take to reduce their impact. First let's look at why car emissions are so high.

Our collective adoration of SUVs means that even though efficiency technology has improved, the average fuel economy per car in the United States actually went *down* from 1987, when it peaked at around 22 miles per gallon (MPG), to 2007, when it was around 21 MPG. If you switch from a normal car to an SUV, the extra energy you'll expend would equal the amount you'd waste if you left your television on for twenty-eight years. That's a long time, yo.

Americans drive an average of 231 miles per week, or about 12,000 miles per year. So assuming the average MPG, they're using about 571 gallons of gas per year. Every gallon of gasoline you use in your car emits about 20 pounds of CO_2. So that means, on average, our cars are emitting 11,420 pounds of CO_2 a year.

Thanks for bearing with me through that calculation. Ah, math. I'll use that number as a basis for calculating some CO_2 savings achieved by implementing the tips in this chapter.

Warning: There's information about car maintenance and driving and fuel economy in here. Maybe that doesn't sound boring to you, but it did to me when I was contemplating researching and writing this chapter. I was surprised to find it's not.

Incidentally, an extensive scientific poll (okay, I asked a bunch of guys over beers one night) suggests that men think it's really cool when chicks know about cars. Actually, who cares if they think it's cool . . . it *is* cool.

DRIVE LESS, WALK MORE

For each mile you don't drive (assuming you're our typical 21 MPG driver), you keep almost a pound of CO_2 out of the atmosphere. It's that simple. You can have fun with this and make a game out of trying to save CO_2, one pound at a time.

It's tough to offer specific advice on this one, because I don't know where or how far you're driving. If your commute to work is 20 miles each way, you're probably not going to walk it. But is there a safe and lovely place to park your car a mile away from work (a mile closer to home, that is)? If so, park there, walk the last mile to and fro, and you've eliminated 2 miles a day—500 pounds of CO_2 per year, assuming you work five days a week and take two weeks vacation, though hopefully you take more vacation than that.

As for other ideas, just start thinking about your driving habits. More than 25 percent of Americans' daily car trips are a mile or shorter. When you run out to the market or coffee shop on weekends, how far away is it? If it's a mile away, and the walk is safe, you could walk instead of drive. Going to hang out with a friend who lives half a mile away? You don't need to drive (and then, if you have a glass of wine or two with that friend, you don't have to worry about getting behind the wheel).

If you live in a city, especially a walking-friendly city, stop driving everywhere. It amazes me how often people in Boston and San Francisco hop in their cars to go places they could *definitely* walk. I don't mean to get up on some high horse (hey! you could ride a horse to work! Kidding . . .). It's as much about saving the hassle of finding a place to park as saving the planet. Walking around a city can be way less stressful. This is coming from someone who kept a car in New York City for six months and drove far more often than necessary, so I know from parking hassles. I love not driving in a city.

Keep track for two or three weeks of all the times you walk instead of drive, and see if it adds up. By then you'll be in the habit. Nice.

Green women don't get fat, part II

For every mile you walk instead of drive, you burn about 100 extra calories. If you do that every day for a week, that's 700 calories. Every day for a year: 36,500 calories. 36,600 calories in a leap year. Woo-hoo. I have no idea if you want to lose weight or not, but if you did this and changed nothing else, you'd lose a little more than ten pounds. (You have to burn 3,600 calories more than you take in to lose a pound.) Bottom line: Unless you start eating way more along with walking an extra mile a day, you won't be getting fat anytime soon.

GET RID OF YOUR CAR— IF YOU CAN

This is a tough one for a lot of people, but think long and hard about it, and if you can be car-free or have your household switch from two cars to one, go for it. If you had asked me three-and-a-half years ago if I would ever get rid of my car, I would have said no way. And I lived in a city and didn't use it every day—or every week, for that matter. Then came the month before my lease was up. (No comments from the peanut gallery about the benefits of buying versus leasing. It's in the past.) I had been traveling for almost a month while parked, unknowingly, in an illegal spot. I returned to a nasty pile of orange parking tickets . . . the amount I had to pay still occasionally gives me nightmares. I decided not to get a new car—just to try it for a month or two. I still don't have one.

At first this took a little getting used to—what about those times when I did need a car? Was I going to feel trapped? I was writing at home about half the time and working from my office at *Boston* magazine the other half of the time, so commuting was not an issue for me. It was a five-second walk to my desk, and a ten-minute walk to the office.

But I still had to figure out what to do when I wanted to leave the city for a weekend getaway or needed to leave the city to research a story about a new luxury spa in Kennebunkport or a hidden gem restaurant in Rhode Island. (You feel sorry for me, don't you?)

The options were many. I could get a ride. I could rent a car (though I think renting a car is one of the biggest pains in the ass ever, and it's always more expensive than you think it will be). I could take the train or the bus. My friend John— who enjoys the finer things in life—let me in on the bus secret. If you find the right bus line, like the one he takes between Boston and Hanover, New Hampshire, it's almost luxurious. The seats are plush, they give you bottled water (not that you should be drinking bottled water), and they show movies.

I have also learned to *love* trains. There's something exciting and romantic about riding the rails. Who am I kidding? Sometimes the commuter rail is crowded, the subway is smelly, and Amtrak is late. But I would rather ride a train than sit in traffic any day. I can zip from the Back Bay in Boston to Penn Station in New York in a little over three hours. I can get from the Upper East Side to Brooklyn in mere minutes. I can avoid getting stuck on San Francisco's Bay Bridge when trying to get to the East Bay for dinner. And you can eliminate traffic hell from your life, too. Anyone who lives outside of a city with a commuter rail system should definitely look into it, and avoid rush-hour stress every day. Trains rock.

For trips where public transport wasn't an option, I discovered Zipcar (zipcar.com). Zipcar may be the best urban transportation innovation ever. There are cars parked all over the city. You reserve one online, go straight to the car, open it with your passcard, and drive away. Gas and insurance are included, so it's never more expensive than you think it's going to be, as long as you're back on time. If not, there's hell to pay. Oh, and the cars? This is the best part. No crappy rental sedans, these. They have sporty Volvos (for when you're in a safe mood), BMWs (for when you're in a snazzy mood), and Mini Coopers (for when you're in a cute, little, British mood). And they have hybrids, which is what I choose most often now.

If you shed a car, you can also bike, carpool (except you won't ever be the one driving, but hey, you're good company and that's contribution enough), walk, or telecommute.

Think about it. Losing one car means losing 11,420 pounds of CO_2 per year. Give it a try.

PIMP YOUR RIDE 🐬

When you gotta drive, you gotta drive. No matter what kind of car you have, there are plenty of things you can do to make it more fuel-efficient. And making your car more fuel-efficient reduces your emissions. If you were getting 20 MPG, for example, and you make your car so fuel-efficient that it gets 25 MPG, instead of emitting 1 pound of CO_2 for every mile, you're now emitting about 0.8 pounds of CO_2 per mile—over the course of 12,000 miles, that's a saving of 2,400 pounds of CO_2. Well done. But how?

Keep your tires pumped up: There's a sticker in your car, probably on the door or doorjamb on the driver's side, that tells you what the pressure in your tires should be. If you can't find it, check the manual. Then fill your tires at least to that point, and maybe a little more, as long as you don't exceed the maximum pressure rating (which should be imprinted on your tires). For every 3 pounds of pressure less than the recommended rating, you lose about 1 percent of your fuel efficiency.

Change your oil regularly: The every 3,000 miles rule that I heard about so often starting when I turned sixteen might be a little stringent, but having it changed every 3,000 to 5,000 miles is a good idea. (As part of a good car maintenance program, this can contribute to 25 percent improvement in fuel efficiency.) Be sure to use your car manufacturer's recommended grade of motor oil. If you change the oil yourself (yeah, right), make sure *not* to dump the oil down a drain or in the trash. The oil from one change can contaminate up to a million gallons of water. Return it in a sealed container to a place that accepts used motor oil (which can be cleaned and reused)—most service stations that sell motor oil will take it back.

Replace your air filters when they're dirty: Make sure to check them monthly and change them about every twelve thousand miles (or sooner if they're dirty). Going from dirty to clean air filters can increase your fuel efficiency by 10 percent.

Get in tune: If you notice that your fuel efficiency has decreased (i.e., you aren't getting as far on a tank of gas), take your ride in for a tune-up. If something major is wrong, getting it fixed could make you up to 40 percent more fuel-efficient.

DRIVE RIGHT

When your car's in tip-top shape and ready to get the most out of its mileage, it's time to put your mad driving skills to the test and make every trip as efficient as possible.

Be smooth: When you're going from zero to sixty—or a stopped position to any speed of motion—do so without slamming on the accelerator. Stop smoothly, too—coast to a halt instead of jamming on the breaks. Finally, when you get going, don't accelerate and decelerate in little bursts. This has always been a huge pet peeve of mine—but more importantly, jerky driving on the highway can make your car about 30 percent less fuel-efficient. So cut it out already.

Stick to the speed limit: Every 5 miles per hour you drive over 60 means you're being 5 or 6 percent less fuel-efficient. Driving faster creates more drag, and as you go faster and faster the drag increases exponentially. Go 75 instead of 55 and you're about 20 percent less efficient. And remember, for all this fuel efficiency stuff, using less gas not only means more CO_2 into the atmosphere, it also means spending more money on gas *and* stopping at smelly gas stations more often. Think speeding is chic? Decidedly not. Safe is the new sexy.

Don't be idle: If you sit still with the car running, you are getting zero miles to the gallon and just burning fuel and emitting CO_2 needlessly. Idling can waste up to ⅜ gallon of gas in thirty minutes. So if, in a given day, you start the car fifteen minutes before you drive it, then later wait for someone for fifteen minutes with the car on, you've emitted as much as 7.5 pounds of CO_2 for no reason at all. If you idle that much even once a week, we're talking about 390 pounds of extra CO_2. If you're going to be stopped for more than thirty seconds, kill the engine.

The AC question

Air conditioning on or off? When it's hot out and you need to keep your car cool and as green as possible, open the windows for fresh air instead of using the AC at speeds of 40 MPH or less. Though using air conditioning can reduce your car's efficiency by 10 percent, when you go faster than 40, the drag created by open windows would outweigh the AC effect. So at that point, windows up and AC on.

KEEP IT NEAT 🜪

Don't use your car as a personal dumping ground. Aside from being aesthetically unpleasing (have you ever gotten into a car that looked like a pigsty inside and thought, wow, this person is super-stylish? Didn't think so), storing excess crap in your car means being less fuel-efficient. An extra 50 pounds means you're 1 percent less fuel-efficient. An extra 100 pounds, my whizzy internal calculator tells me, means you're 2 percent less efficient. Which means, in our average driving scenario, an extra 200-plus pounds of CO_2 emitted over the course of a year.

Speaking as someone who did occasionally—or almost always—let the mess in her car get out of control, I offer this advice: Don't let it pile up. Cleaning out one day's worth or one weekend's worth of gear and refuse should be easy, but tackling a year's accumulation of stuff is daunting. Scan the scene before you exit stage left and if there's stuff there that shouldn't be, take it with you *immediately* and put it away.

Safety bonus: Having things in the back of your car that aren't strapped down is dangerous. Not to scare you, but they can act as projectile weapons if you have to slam on the brakes or if you get into an accident. And nobody likes projectile weapons.

Tip: To reduce your weight and your wind resistance further, remove ski and bike racks when you're not using them. If you don't feel like taking them off and putting them back on with every trip, at least make sure they're off when the season ends.

IF YOU'RE IN THE MARKET FOR A NEW CAR, GO HYBRID

I was in Los Angeles for New Year's Eve this year and let me tell you: Hybrids are everywhere. Specifically, the Toyota Prius. It is *the* cool car to drive. Anyone who's anyone has one. This is such a better trend than skinny jeans. (No one looks good in skinny jeans.)

So what the heck does hybrid mean? With cars, it refers to the combination of an electric motor that's powered by an onboard rechargeable battery and a fuel-powered engine. Hybrids get much better gas mileage than standard cars for several reasons. The gas engine isn't running all the time, because the electric engine can take over; the engine is smaller and lighter and, therefore, the car is lighter; a hybrid may capture some of the energy given off as heat when you break and return it to the engine; many hybrids are made of light-weight materials, so the whole car is lighter and therefore requires less energy to accelerate or climb hills; many hybrids are also aerodynamically designed to reduce drag.

All this results in amazing gas mileage. The Toyota Prius can get 60 MPG in the city and 51 on the highway (yes, some hybrids get better mileage driving in the city, where they might use the electric motor more). The Honda Insight can get 61 in the city and 68 on the highway. Still lusting for an SUV? The two-door Ford Escape gets 36 in the city and 31 on the highway, and the Lexus RX 400h (aren't you the fancy pants?) gets 31 in the city and 27 on the highway. (Ahem. This is not *really* a great green option. But it's better than a Hummer.) For the high rollers who want options, Porsche is planning to release a hybrid in '08; for the anti-high rollers, Chevy's got a hybrid Malibu. I wonder if there will be a hybrid Malibu Barbie soon?

Feeling used

If you don't want to pony up for a hybrid ride—hybrids usually start in the low to mid-20s, and Lexus hybrids are hella more than that—get a used car instead of a brand new one. The production of a new car emits an average of eight thousand pounds of CO_2 (plus hundreds of pounds of other pollutants).

DON'T WASH IT YOURSELF

Taking a spin through the car wash is more ecofriendly than washing your wheels yourself. This one surprised me, and (because I no longer own a car and am out of the car-washing loop) I only thought about it when my brother, Seth, called me from his car, just outside of the car wash, to ask me if he should proceed.

So I did a little quickie research and told him to drive ahead when the little green light came on. The average home car wash uses more than 115 gallons of water; car wash places use much less (more than 60 percent less) than that anyway *and* recapture some of it for reuse. What they don't recapture gets treated in some way to be less environmentally offensive. I'm assuming you don't have a mechanism in place to treat the stuff you rinse off in your driveway or on your lawn. If you must wash at home, use completely biodegradable soap, and don't leave the hose running the whole time. Fill a bucket or two instead, and keep the water off as much as you can.

I must admit I was relieved to learn that car washes are the preferred method of cleaning vehicles. I love going to the car wash. It's like your car is about to be eaten by a giant monster but you're safe inside and you make a daring escape at the last minute. Yes, I know that's weird. But I bet you've thought the same thing.

From getting around to getting away: Ten travel tips

There are some people who will tell you that being ecofriendly requires avoiding travel as much as possible. I am not one of those people. Yes, the transportation generally involved with travel (read: airplanes) is a big contributor to global warming and pollution. But I believe in exploring the world as much as possible to gain an appreciation for this vast, amazing place we want to preserve, as long as we do it as lightly and greenly as possible.

1. Think before you fly

Again, I'm not going to advocate cutting out flying altogether, or skipping "unnecessary" leisure travel if it requires a flight. But we should consider alternatives before we hop on a plane—and see if we can fly at least a little less, and choose to take trains or other forms of public transportation. The reason flying is such a concern for environmentalists is because airplanes generate more than 600 million tons of CO_2 per year, accounting for about 3 percent of total CO_2

emissions. And because they also emit a lot of stuff besides CO_2, most notably NO_2 and water vapors, planes' overall contribution to global warming weighs in more heavily, at about 9 percent. The flights most important—and most practical—to eliminate are those shorter than 500 miles. The most fuel is used on flights during takeoff and landing—so two short flights would burn more fuel and have more emissions than a long flight of equal or longer total distance. For flights longer than 500 miles, the emissions per mile for a passenger on a commercial airplane are comparable to emissions for car travel.

Tip: Forego the private jet, dahling. Flying commercial is way more ecofriendly, because all the fuel burned transports hundreds of people, not just a few.

2. Offset your travel

It's not a perfect solution, but offsetting travel does help to alleviate some of the strain planes, trains, and automobiles put on the planet. It works more or less like this: You use a carbon calculator, which most offset companies provide online, to figure out how much CO_2 your travel effectively emitted. Then you pay the appropriate amount to "offset" those emissions to a company that's investing in sustainable energy, such as wind power or solar power, or making other efforts to reduce greenhouse gases in the environment, such as planting trees. (A tree can absorb about 26 pounds of CO_2 in a year.) It's not expensive to do this. At Terrapass (terrapass.com), for example, you can offset 6,000 miles of flying (round-trip from coast to coast) for $9.95. Some offset companies are for-profit; others are nonprofit—they can both be effective, but you should be aware that many offset companies aren't just in it for the planet. Start reading on page 193 for the names of a offset companies I like. Note: Airplane travel has become a popular area to offset; you can offset car miles and general living emissions, too.

3. Practice conscious plane behavior

Remember that the rules of conservation that apply on the ground also apply at 30,000 feet:

- Bring your own cup for flight attendants to fill with water.
- Decline napkins and those individual servings of processed snack mix. (Chic bonus: Airplane snack mixes are almost always flavored with garlic powder, so avoiding them means fresher breath when you emerge from several hours on a plane.)
- Say no to soda—but if you're dying to quench your thirst with something in a can while you're on the plane, take the can with you off the plane and recycle it. U.S. airports and airlines throw away enough aluminum cans each year to build fifty-eight 747 airplanes.
- Recycle any magazines or newspapers that you bring on board.
- Don't overuse paper towels in the lavatory.
- Speaking of the lavatory, one Chinese airline recently began asking passengers to go at home and hold it on the plane because each flush burns extra fuel and costs the airline more (and might emit 14 pounds of CO_2, but that's not what they were worried about).

Whatever the number is, just in case it's true—and because airplane bathrooms don't smell very good and are germ havens— keep your trips to the loo to a minimum.

4. Pack light
Aim to bring only carry-on bags with you on airplane flights. This has multiple green benefits. First, it will encourage you to pack lighter, which means you'll be more thoughtful about bringing outfits you love. Oh, and less weight on a plane means less fuel burned. (An extra 10 pounds of weight per passenger equals an increase in CO_2 emissions of more than 3.5 million tons in a year.) Plus, airlines sometimes lose bags. I almost never check bags, but the last three times I did? Lost. Which means you'll either have to buy new stuff to get you through the trip (not green) or wear the same outfit for days on end (not chic or pleasant for those within nose-shot).

5. Choose destinations where it's easy (or at least possible) to be green
You don't have to restrict all your travel time to environmental volun-teerism (though that is a cool thing to do on vaca), but pick places to visit where you won't stress yourself out because it's so impos-sible to be even the palest shade of green. (Las Vegas comes to mind . . . it's not a place you want to walk around outside, someone needs to tell them to shut off the lights, and just try to find an intimate restaurant serving only food from local farms.) Look for cities where walking is appealing, public transportation is easy, or biking is a typical way to get around (go to Europe for that). Or plan a trip to a

fabulous eco-resort in a stunning natural setting. Check out respon-sibletravel.com to find one; the same website offers ideas for volun-teer conservation travel, too.

6. Don't rent a car when you get there

If you don't absolutely need it, skip the car rental when you travel. If you do rent a car, you may feel compelled to use it and not seek out alternatives. And there are definitely alternatives, including public transportation, walking, and biking. European cities from Barcelona to Oslo are incredibly bike-friendly, and there are options galore for renting bikes. Walking is the best way to get to know a new place, whether it's a tiny village or a huge city. And figuring out the local public transportation system is always easier than figuring out how and where to drive in a foreign land. Even if that foreign land is, say, Cincinnati. Of course, there are parts of the planet that you can't access by train or plane and some sort of car or van trans-port is necessary. In those cases, work with a local transportation company to get you where you want to be—one with a record of treading lightly. (If they are environmentally sensitive, their website will tell you.) Once you reach your destination, explore it on your own power if you can.

Green women don't get fat, part III

Part of the joy of traveling is eating, especially when you're in a place with some funky (in a good way) cuisine. Diets do not belong on vacation. Having said that, you don't want to return home with extra baggage in the form of flab. That will just stress you out, and then all your good vacation karma goes bye-bye. If you get around on your own power (walking, biking, or hiking), you won't need to worry. You'll likely be in motion way more than you are at home. If you cover four miles on foot and bike another ten, even at a totally vacation-relaxed pace, you've burned about 700 calories. If you start the day with a three-mile jog (my personal favorite way to explore a new place early in the morning), you're at 1,000 calories scorched. Bon appetit.

7. Choose green chic hotels

Support hotels that practice energy conservation or use alternative energy (such as wind or solar energy) for at least part of their power, that save water through linen reuse programs and efficient laundry practices, and that have recycling programs in place. Also look for hotels that use ecofriendly cleaning products, furniture, and linens. These days, if a hotel is actively practicing environmentalism, the staff will know about it—so ask when you call to make a reservation or check out their websites to see if it's touted. Well-known chic hotel chains pursuing impressive green initiatives include Kimpton Hotels (kimptonhotels.com) and Fairmont Hotels & Resorts (fairmont.com). To find the greenest hotels in the city of your choice, visit greenhotels.com (not the chicest-looking website, but some fab hotels). Go to page 193 to read about a few of my favorite green chic hotels.

8. Keep up the green in your home away from home

It's not just up to the hotel to be green. You need to practice green habits on the road as well as at home. Take part in linen reuse programs and don't ask to have your sheets and towels changed every day. Don't drink the bottled water. Time your shower and keep it short. Shut off the lights, air conditioner, and television when you leave the room. Don't take the extra little bottles of shampoo and conditioner if they're unopened—then the hotel will have to replace them for the next guest, and somewhere a factory making those tiny plastic bottles will have to make an extra set. Do take the partially used ones home if you'll finish the product and recycle the bottle.

9. Be a savvy souvenir shopper

Purchase only beautiful items that you love and can't get anywhere else and that didn't cause any damage to the environment. Most of the crap we buy on vacation is . . . well, crap. So don't buy it. Lugging a too-heavy bag is not chic at all—my image of the sophisticated traveler is a well-dressed woman with one shoulder bag and a neat little carry-on, casually breezing through the airport. (Somehow I don't ever get that look down—I always end up looking a little disheveled at the airport. But I try.) Anyway, don't add weight to your bag (see tip #4 in this section) unless you're buying something you really want, like an item handcrafted with indigenous materials by a local artisan. Skip the plastic tchotchkes (you know how I feel about plastic and tchotchkes) and avoid products made with parts of endangered species (ivory, tortoise shell, animal skins, etc.).

10. Leave things green at home

Coming home to a flooded basement is so not the way to keep the happy vacation mode going. But that doesn't mean you need to leave your heat cranking. Here are a few things to take care of before you hit the road.

- Turn your water heater down to low.
- Set your heat at a level warm enough to keep your pipes from freezing in winter, but no warmer.
- Unplug your television, DVD player, computer, and small appliances (blender, toaster, coffeemaker), which draw energy even when they aren't in use.
- Have someone water your plants so they keep cleaning your indoor air (and so they don't die).
- If you still get a newspaper delivered daily, stop it while you're gone—and consider donating it. The *New York Times* offers a vacation donation program—the value of your week's or two week's worth of papers is put toward a subscription for a school.

Chapter Eight

ON OCCASIONS

Entertaining, gift-giving, and celebrating birthdays, the holidays, and weddings can bring up a host of environmental faux pas if you're not careful. Does that mean you should stop throwing chic soirees, cancel the surprise bash for your best friend, and give up the fun when 'tis the season? What do you think? Hells no.

But you gotta take a look at how you're making merry. When we celebrate, we go nuts. Even if we're greenish most of the time, we throw all the rules out the window when it's party time. We throw out mad trash and food, too. Between Thanksgiving and New Year's Day—the most celebration-heavy period of the year—we toss an extra *million* tons of garbage each week.

In the midst of all that crumpled wrapping paper, stale pie, and disposable flatware, doesn't it seem like a less-is-more mentality about celebrating would be nice? A little calmer, a little more focused on what's important (no, *not* getting the package with the biggest bow): spending time with friends and family and just *enjoying*. The outstanding thing is that par-tays with less junk cluttering them tend to be more beautiful and more fun. I don't have a statistic to back that up. (Can you measure beauty and fun-ness?) But speaking from the experience of going to parties, dozens upon dozens of dinners, and more weddings than I care to count, it's true.

SEND GREEN CARDS 🌿

I'm torn on the topic of invitations. The most ecofriendly way to invite people to your next divine affair is via Evite. But Evite just doesn't go with a divine affair. Don't get me wrong: I love Evite. For some things.

But for many holiday parties, engagement parties, showers, weddings, and such, getting a lovely invitation in the mail is, well, quite lovely. And when it's time to send a holiday card or birthday card? The electronic greeting basically says, "Uh oh, I totally forgot to get you a card but here is my pathetic last-second effort. Love ya!" Not a fan.

What gives me pause, though, is that every pound of virgin paper made from tree pulp means about 1 pound of CO_2 is emitted. (The paper industry, which I discuss in more detail on page 36, is the third largest industrial emitter of greenhouse gases.) Which may not sound like all that much, but around the holidays about 2.6 billion cards are sent. Now, let's assume each of those weighs 0.5 ounces. (The U.S. Post Office requires only one stamp on any letter weighing 1 ounce or less; I've gotten some thick holiday cards and wedding invitations that required extra postage, and so obviously weigh more than 1 ounce; 0.5 seems like a nice conservative estimate.) That would be 81.25 million pounds of paper, and if all that paper is virgin paper, 81.25 million pounds of CO_2.

Yikes. But even knowing that number doesn't make me want to send a heartfelt e-card to a close friend on the occasion of her birthday or engagement, or an Evite to my wedding. Luckily, there are ecofriendly paper options, and I endorse these wholeheartedly for formal invitations, holiday cards, and birthdays. At a minimum, look for cards and invitations made at least partly from recycled materials. Optimally, you'll find paper made from 100 percent postconsumer recycled papers. (Most of those will say so on the back.) Ask your local paper shop what totally recycled lines they carry, and request more.

And think outside the wood pulp. Paper made from cotton is gorgeous, and while organic cotton paper is the ideal, most cotton paper, including beautiful cotton papers from Crane's (crane.com) is made with waste from the textile industry, making it an eco-friendlier choice than virgin paper. Kenaf and hemp papers are also good, because kenaf and hemp plants are sustainable and easy to grow without pesticides. Look for a cool selection of recycled and tree-free papers at Vickerey (vickerey.com).

A note on thank-you notes: This is getting away from green living and into just being nice, but if you've been a guest at a dinner party or someone's weekend home (lucky), a thank-you of some sort is in order. Not via email. Always send a note, and always do it on the most ecofriendly stationery you can find.

Tip: Avoid cards that have been embedded with metallic spark-lies or coated in plastic. The melding of different types of material makes them tough (or impossible) to recycle. They're probably tacky, too.

RETHINK REFRESHMENTS 🍸

Food and booze are key elements of good parties. (Genius observation, yes? Martha Stewart has nothing on me.) Food and booze also tend to get served in excess and often wasted, and make up a huge part of all the party-related garbage. More than 25 percent of the food produced for humans in the United States gets thrown out—that's almost 50 million tons of food annually. Over the course of a year, if you cut down the stuff you throw away by just 25 percent, you'd keep the equivalent of 1,000 pounds of CO_2 a year out of the atmosphere. That's because landfills are a major source of anthropogenic methane (that's methane derived from human activity, but I wanted to sound smart and say "anthropogenic")—they're responsible for about 34 percent of all human-initiated methane emissions—and methane is a greenhouse gas twenty-three times more potent than CO_2 in its contribution to global warming.

So don't make more food than you need. Buffet-style setups are the biggest food wasters, because you have to make enough of every dish for every guest, and you have way more than you need. Go for a reasonably portioned sit-down dinner or brunch (it doesn't have to be formal—you can do it family style).

Or maybe you just want to do cocktails and passed hors d'oeuvres. If that's the case, think about the time of day and how hungry people will be. Assuming appies that can be consumed in a bite or two (and that's how they should be or it gets messy), aim for three to five pieces per person for a predinner party; six to eight pieces per person for a party later in the evening (when some guests will have eaten and some will not); and ten to twelve pieces per person if you're having heavy hors d'oeuvres right around dinnertime and you think not many people will have eaten elsewhere.

Use as many local and organic ingredients as you can. If you're working with a caterer, make sure they understand how important being green is to you. Even if she isn't a strictly ecofriendly caterer, any good caterer will be happy to source ingredients locally, eliminate as much waste as possible, recycle waste and compost leftovers, and use cloth napkins and china instead of disposables.

Tip: Contact local shelters to find out if you can donate leftovers, and what their criteria are for accepting food. No one wants your Uncle Joe's scraps.

Cheers

Serve organic wine and beer (read more about why on page 73) and make organic cocktails, too. Use organic vodka and organic gin— if you're thinking , "why does that matter?", remember that spirits are derived from plants, and it takes a lot of plants to make a lot of spirits, and the plants used to make organic spirits are grown without chemical pesticides and fertilizers. Better for the planet, better for you—except for the whole hangover thing. Some people think hangovers aren't as bad with organic booze, but this is still alcohol, people.

Square One Vodka (squareonevodka.com) is made from organically grown American rye (using a certified organic fermentation process); Juniper Green Organic London Dry Gin (junipergreen.org) is made from organic juniper, organic coriander, organic angelica, and organic savory.

Tip: Craft creative cocktails (alliteration is fun . . . or maybe I need to stop doing shots of organic vodka) using organic fruit purees and herb infusions instead of processed syrups to complete the organic effect. For inspiration, read the cocktail menu from Cyrus, a fabulous restaurant in Healdsburg, California (it's online; cyrusrestaurant.com). Cyrus bar master Scott Beattie is a genius. If you happen to be in Wine Country anytime soon, go in, say hi, and be sure to have a drink.

LET THERE BE (LED) LIGHT

Strands of shiny little holiday lights are awesome, except that the normal ones use quite a bit of excess energy. If you've decorated a tree, for example, with a string of three hundred mini-incandescent lights, you'll use about 30 kilowatt-hours of energy (emitting about 45 pounds of extra CO_2) over the holiday season. If you use those big fat holiday lights, we're talking more than 450 kilowatt-hours and close to 700 pounds of CO_2. The mini lights are the preferable choice, and even better is a string of LED lights. They're available at Target,

Costco, and Lowe's, and though they cost more than incandescents (a string of 100 LED lights will run you $10 to $15), they last forever. Okay, not forever, but fifty thousand hours. And they use about 10 percent of the energy of the mini incandescents—less than 3 kilowatt-hours throughout the holidays. Plus, they don't get hot, meaning your fire risk goes down.

Tip: You could skip the Christmas tree altogether. But I don't do that, so I'm not going to tell you to do it. Besides, buying a tree from the right place could actually mean *supporting* the environment and your community. Choose a tree from a small, local farm that grows them sustainably. If that's not an option, get one in a pot that can be replanted. If yours is a cut tree, don't trash it—find out how and where it can be recycled and **take it down before the deadline.** Many cities and towns will only accept trees until sometime in early January. Which is a good thing, because a droopy, needle-dropping tree that's still up in March is not chic.

WRAP IT UP

Because of the large quantities of ink used in printing and the low quality of the paper fibers, regular gift wrap is often not recyclable. Nor is most gift wrap made from recycled materials. I think I may have mentioned before (pages 36 and 164) that the production of virgin paper is a tad energy intensive (and associated with the ills of rapid deforestation), so using up virgin paper on something that's going to be torn off a gift in ten seconds and tossed away seems like a bad idea. Let me take a firmer stance: It is a bad idea, especially when there are alternatives. If you want to wrap a gift in paper, look for papers made from postconsumer recycled paper or tree-free materials like hemp. Paporganics (paporganics.com) makes a beautiful line of papers that are 90 percent postconsumer paper and 10 percent hemp, and dyed with vegetable-based inks. Consider alternatives to paper, too. This is the time to get creative. Use an organic cotton or linen napkin tied up with ribbon (try raffia ribbon instead of synthetic). Instead of a disposable gift bag (again, not so recyclable), how about a canvas bag that the lucky recipient can reuse for shopping—or returning the gift?

Tip: It's great to save ribbon and boxes that you might reuse as gift wrap, but pack rats are creepy. Do not become that crazy lady who saves every last scrap of string. That's not becoming. Let the crud go. Be a discerning saver, and you'll have a go-to collection of pretty wrapping supplies. My favorite combo of late is clear cellophane bags (you always end up with some of these from somewhere) with colored tissue paper (saved from another gift or made from recycled paper) wrapped around the gift inside the bag, which is tied with just a bit of elegant ribbon (that I kept from another gift). Oohs and ahs every time. You hear me knockin,' Martha?

Give green gifts

When choosing gifts, don't automatically default to things. Most people don't need more things. And if you give them things they don't like or already have, it's uncomfortable for everyone. Unless you know exactly what someone wants or needs, think about alternatives to things. Like what? Good question. I love giving gift certificates. Not impersonal ones, but thoughtfully chosen ones. For a friend who adores a certain yoga studio? A 10-class pass. A foodie couple who just got married? Dinner at a hidden gem restaurant. For the gal who has (and can easily afford) everything? A donation to a charity that is especially meaningful to her. A ballet lover? Tickets. (See, this isn't so hard.) A friend who's been working like crazy and totally stressed out? Massage at her favorite spa. And just hope that she reciprocates.

Ten ecofriendly gift ideas, for everyone:
1. **For your mom:** Her favorite photo of you and your sibs, and a gift certificate to a shop that carries beautiful frames made from reclaimed materials, like the frames by Dryads Dancing (dryads-dancing.com)
2. **For your dad:** A gift certificate to his favorite bookstore
3. **For your bro:** Front-row tickets to his favorite team's home game
4. **For your sis:** A pedi, or a private pilates package (or front-row tickets to her favorite team's home game)
5. **For your BFF:** A girls' getaway night at your favorite (green) luxury hotel
6. **For your rock-and-roll s.o.:** A vintage guitar
7. **For your sporty s.o.:** Sessions with a private trainer or top-notch instructor in a favorite sport
8. **For your single self:** An ecofriendly vibrator (yes, ma'am) from

Jimmy Jane (jimmyjane.com)

9. For the happy couple: A bottle of biodynamic wine from the place they were married (or had their honeymoon)

10. For your wedding guests: Plant trees (a tree for every guest) in their honor

DO A GREEN CLEANUP

Even if you're overwhelmed by a post-party mess, stick with your green cleaning routine. (Hopefully, cutting down on waste, which is a big point in this chapter in case you missed it, means the mess is less overwhelming than it might otherwise have been.)

Use ecofriendly cleaning products and reusable cloth rags, and don't leave the water running the whole time you're cleaning. Recycle your wine and beer bottles. If your city doesn't accept wine bottles for recycling, some wineries will take back used wine bottles—check with a winery near you. And there is a winery near you—there are now wineries in all fifty states. If you want to recycle the corks, too, check out Yemm & Hart's cork-recycling program (yemmhart.com).

What you can't recycle may end up in a trash bag. Make the sack itself as ecofriendly as possible: Look for bags made from recycled plastic, such as Seventh Generation (seventhgen.com). If every U.S. household replaced twenty virgin plastic bags with twenty bags made from even 65 percent recycled materials, that would save more than forty-five thousand barrels of oil (that's enough to heat and cool 2,500 homes for a year). Or try a completely biodegradable and compostable bag such as those from BioBag (biogroupusa.com). They're derived from cornstarch instead of petroleum.

Tip: Don't do disposables. To lighten your waste load, refrain from using disposable plastic plates, napkins, cups, and flatware. If you need more dishes and linens to take care of your guests, check out cool antique and vintage stores first. (Don't bother going into crappy vintage stores with dust-covered wares and nothing that looks remotely appealing. If you like the displays in the windows and the vibe of the shop, you'll probably have better luck.) If you buy new, get napkins in organic or renewable fabrics—rawganique.com has a big selection. For other tableware and serving pieces, look for materials such as recycled glass, sustainable woods, and ceramics colored with nontoxic dyes. Vivaterra.com is my favorite online source for all that stuff.

WHEN YOU WED... 🍂

I'm going to keep this section short and sweet, because not everyone is planning a wedding at the moment. But 2.4 million couples in the United States are, and the wedding has morphed into the mother of all occasions. The guidelines in this section apply as much to weddings as to last-minute dinner parties— maybe more, because weddings tend to be so over-the-top (when was the last time you spend $50,000 . . . or much, much more . . . on a casual dinner party?). If you're getting married, vow to do it greenly. (I had to use some kind of vow pun. It was

either "vow to do it greenly" or "say 'I do' to a green wedding."
Which do you like better?)

Quick tips in addition to what I've already covered here:

- Keep it on the small, intimate side (more guests = more waste).
- Don't bother with ginormous centerpieces but choose simple, gorgeous, local flowers, preferably organic, instead.
- Rather than register for china you'll never use and glasses you'll be afraid might break, register for donations to a special charity.
- Replace favors with a donation to your favorite charity in guests' names, or offset the miles they traveled to watch you wed (for more on offsets, see page 156).
- Pick a venue where it's easy being green (an ecofriendly resort or a nature preserve-type place that will benefit from the money you're spending on location).
- Above all, remember that the point of a wedding is to marry your beloved in the presence of those near and dear to you. It's not about the stuff (dress, gifts, place, cards) at all.

Congratulations. I wish you a beautiful wedding and an even beautiful-er marriage.

Eco-etiquette

Thoughts of weddings often lead me to thoughts of etiquette. The point of etiquette is not to follow some antiquated rules of decorum for no good reason. It's about interacting in a way that makes others feel at ease. I didn't make that up. Peter Post, Emily Post's great-grandson, told me that one time when I interviewed him for a story. I arrived late to that interview. Can you believe that? I was late to an interview with Peter Post. Oops. He was ever so gracious. And that's good etiquette.

Anyway, when it comes to living an ecofriendly lifestyle and expressing your opinions about it, be gracious. If someone you know drinks bottled water or uses incandescent lightbulbs or throws a five-hundred-guest wedding, it's not because she hates the planet and wants the glaciers to melt and animals to perish. She probably just doesn't know what's up.

If you'd like to share some thoughts, broach the subject gently. It's beyond splendid to spread the green chic word, but do so without pushing, judging, or insisting that your way is best. (By the way, I'm reminding myself this as much as anything.) Share your excitement about all the changes individuals can easily and stylishly make, not your criticism of the way others live their lives. If someone happens to give you a nongreen gift, don't throw it against a wall and walk away in disgust like you did when your boyfriend gave you a Cincinnati Bengals T-shirt for your birthday. (Oh, wait. That was me.) Don't say things to make her feel bad. Say thank you, and if you don't want it, find somewhere to donate it. Next time you see her, start easing her into ideas of ecofriendliness. Oh, and recommend this book to everyone you know. Now that is excellent eco-etiquette.

Chapter Nine

BIG GREEN THINGS

Thanks for reading the whole book (or for skipping ahead to the last chapter so you could pretend you read it). May I offer some final words of wisdom? Do not sweat every single tiny decision you make. You'll go nutty as you stand in the supermarket trying to decide if it's better to buy shampoo in a bottle made from 50 percent postconsumer waste or 100 percent non-postconsumer recycled materials. You'll develop a complex if you feel guilty every time you turn on the lights or throw something away. This will stress you out. And stress doesn't make you look good, as we covered on page 112. So I'll say again: Relax. Ah.

Rather than get lost in minutiae, the key to green living is shifting your mindset so you incorporate conscious living broadly into every part of your life—then an occasional not-perfectly-green decision won't really matter. Instead of fretting over which shampoo bottle to buy, congratulate yourself for being aware enough to buy something consciously in a recycled package, pick the one that smells best, and move on.

In general, some of the big areas to focus on include the following:

- Consume (buy) only what you truly need or love.
- Drive less, and when you do drive, drive more fuel-efficiently.
- Make your home greener, healthier, chemical-free, and more energy-efficient.
- Eat as many local, organic, whole foods that don't come in packages as you can.
- Avoid synthetic chemicals as much as possible.
- Support local farmers, designers, and shops.
- Support companies that use ecofriendly practices and are coming up with innovative ways to make green products.
- Talk to people in your community about ways to make it more ecofriendly—from neighborhood cleanups to tree plantings to building bike paths.
- Reduce the amount of stuff and packaging you acquire and throw away.
- Reuse the things that are worth reusing (and safe to reuse).
- Recycle as much of everything else as possible.
- Create more demand (and close the loop on the recycling process) by buying recycled products.
- Get some sleep and take care of yourself.
- Celebrate and enjoy the world—and you'll be more in tune with the place you're striving to save.

I know that's still a lot to remember, but as with anything, it just takes a little practice. Remember the first time you rode a bike or had sex? It was probably a little daunting and nerve-wracking. But now (hopefully!) it's all good—just something you do and love. Green chic living can be just like that. So just start doing it.

Chapter Ten

MY FAVORITE GREEN THINGS

This is not a comprehensive list of every green thing out there. It is, as the title so wittily suggests, a list of my very favorite chic green things. (In case you were wondering, a product that's green is not necessarily chic. Though green and not chic is chicer than not green and not chic. Just saying.) So anyway, these are my faves.

Little things

L.L. Bean Boat & Tote bags
llbean.com
Okay, I know these aren't made from organic cotton, but they last *forever* and they always look good.

Sigg

mysigg.com

Practically indestructible—and snazzy looking—stainless steel water bottles.

Gorgeous things

Burt's Bees

burtsbees.com

Everything from pretty tinted lip shimmers to chemical-free sunscreen, all in super-ecofriendly packaging.

Farmaesthetics

farmaesthetics.com

Amazing skin care products and lotions. The Sweet Milk Facial Exfoliate (made with nothing more than powdered milk, fine cornmeal, and organic lavender, chamomile, and orange peel) will make you glow. The (very chic) packaging is as minimal and recyclable as possible, and the company uses solar heating in their office and warehouse. Love.

International Orange

internationalorange.com

My home away from home in San Francisco, this beautiful and serene spa-slash-yoga studio utilizes ecofriendly mats and props and offers spa treatments (the massages are *heavenly*) and facials incorporating products made from natural ingredients. The lounge has little chunks of organic dark chocolate to snack on.

Jāsön

jason-natural.com

Fantastic sunscreens and skin care products that will make you glow. My face is ever so grateful that I discovered this line.

Juice Beauty

juicebeauty.com

My skin needs face products that *work*. Juice Beauty does the trick. This is serious skin care with healthy ingredients. The Green Apple line has hydroxy acids derived from apple, lemon, and raw sugar.

Pangea Organics

pangeaorganics.com

Awesome skin care products and soaps and lotions and stuff.

Preserve Triple Razor

recycline.com

The handle's made from recycled #5 plastic. The triple blade will get your legs silky smooth. It will even work on your boyfriend's thickest stubble.

Style things

4 March

4march.com

Two young designers in Boston recently launched this sophisticated line of clothes made from organic cotton, tussah silk, banana silk, and alpaca.

Charmone

charmoneshoes.com

Think of Charmone as the green Manolo. Gorgeous, sexy, non-leather, PVC-free shoes that are pricey but so worth the splurge.

Envi

shopenvi.com

A smashing boutique in Boston opened in 2007 by two Tufts grads. They carry ecofriendly lines like Stewart+Brown, Twice Shy, and Del Forte.

Gomi NYC

gominyc.com

Tiny and steadfastly cutting-edge, this East Village boutique has been ecofriendly and fabulous since 2003.

Greenloop

thegreenloop.com

An online source for all things eco-stylish: Loomstate and Del Forte denim, Nature vs. Future, Undesigned by Carol Young, and much more.

Green With Glamour

greenwithglamour.com

A well-curated collection of ecofriendly clothes, accessories, and home goods.

Levi's

levi.com

The most classically chic of all denim companies recently introduced a flattering organic cotton line.

Nau

nau.com

Sleek outdoor wear (and some indoor wear, too) made from advanced ecofriendly fabrics. This isn't your hippie sister's green gear.

Pangaya

pangaya.com

A reliably stylish online eco-fashion resource.

Patagonia

patagonia.com

The sweetest outdoor gear around. It's technically superior and looks great, plus Patagonia is beyond committed to sustainability. The products reflect that—all cotton is organic, and many base layers are made from recycled polyester.

Sodafine

sodafine.com

Some green grows in Brooklyn. In addition to shops in Williamsburg and Park Slope, this purveyor of sustainable fashions from Bahar Shahpar, She-Bible, Loyale.

Stewart + Brown

stewartbrown.com

My fashion obsession. I cannot tell you how much I adore this line. S+B's sexy cashmere sweaters, organic cotton tees, cashmere accessories, and silk-hemp dresses and camis are all about sustainability.

Home things

Branch

branchhome.com

Fabulously design-conscious, Branch elevates home décor to the uber-stylish stratosphere.

eConscious Market

econsciousmarket.com

Fifty percent of the proceeds from sales of home accessories (mod lights; Esque recycled glassware), apparel (Moral Fervor; signature organic cotton "Giving. It's the New Getting" tees), and more go to nonprofit organizations—you get to choose which.

Furnature

furnature.com

Classic, sophisticated sofas, loveseats, upholstered benches for a grown-up apartment (or house). All nontoxic with no VOCs or formaldehyde, and organic fabrics available.

Loop

looporganic.com

Clean, classic, luxe organic cotton sheets, blankets, and towels—the whites are bleached without chlorine, and the colors, like chocolate brown and robin's egg blue, all come from low-impact dyes.

Method

methodhome.com

The best-smelling and most effective home cleaning products (from Grapefruit spray cleaner to Fresh Air detergent). The packaging is ecofriendly and chic and the price is right.

Mod Green Pod

modgreenpod.com

Organic cotton fabrics and PVC-free wallpaper in fabulous patterns.

Mrs. Meyer's Clean Day

mrsmeyers.com

Well-priced, ecofriendly dishwashing liquid, wood cleaners, tub scrubs, and more in lavender, lemon verbena, and geranium scents.

Old Fashioned Milk Paint

milkpaint.com

Milk-based paints in perfect historic hues. More expensive than regular paint but not crazy: a pint is $9.95; a gallon is $45.95.

Q Collection

qcollection.com

Gorgeous furniture with nontoxic finishes and sustainable fabrics.

Spring

astorecalledspring.com

This San Francisco store, which has online shopping available, carries all (chic) ecofriendly home stuff, from cleaning supplies to luxurious sheets and towels.

Vivetique

Vivetique.com

Healthy, super-comfy, and supportive green mattresses.

Dining and drinking things

American Flatbread

americanflatbread.com

This Vermont-based pizza-maker has a few restaurants around the country (which are always fun and laid-back), and they also make the most outstanding (organic) frozen pizzas ever, working in regional bakeries so they don't have to ship very far.

American Seasons

Americanseasons.com

My favorite restaurant on Nantucket, a place loaded with excellent restaurants. American Seasons revolves around seasonal food, serves local beer and vodka, and sources wine from organic and biodynamic vineyards.

Blue Hill
Bluehillnyc.com
Even in winter in Manhattan, chef Dan Barber sources as many foods as possible from farms within 200 miles of the restaurant. Have this morning's farm egg as an appetizer. That's a good egg. (Get it? Good egg. You're almost done here—no more puns.)

Boloco
boloco.com
My favorite burrito chain in Boston just went green: stringent recycling program, eco-friendlier packaging, hormone- and antibiotic-free meats.

Chez Panisse
chezpanisse.com
If Alice Waters hadn't opened Chez Panisse in 1971, there's no way American chefs today would be as committed to local and sustainable foods as they are now. Call a month in advance to reserve your spot. The food is so amazing here it brought a little tear to my eye.

Dagoba Chocolate
dagobachocolate.com
Outstanding organic chocolate—good for eating and baking— from a company that's way committed to sustainability.

Farmers Diner

farmersdiner.com

Sometimes you need diner food. And if the urge strikes when you're in Vermont, head to the Farmers Diner, where practically everything is sourced locally. And soooo yummy.

The Herb Farm

theherbfarm.com

One of Seattle's longstanding shmanciest restaurants, this place keeps you in your seat for nine fabulous courses, and you won't want to leave. It's not stuffy, though: You can wear what you want, but if you go on Halloween, costumes are mandatory.

The Kitchen

kitchencafe.com

Even the takeout containers are biodegradable at this environmentally sensitive Boulder eatery. But that's not why it's often called one of the best restaurants in Colorado. The food rocks.

L'Espalier

lespalier.com

The best fancy restaurant in Boston. Chef Frank McClelland has been using seasonal, local, organic ingredients since long before it was trendy. And he grows his own organic herbs and greens on the roof. (Plants on the roof in a city are a very green thing.)

Lumiere

lumiererestaurant.com

Just outside Boston, Michael Levitan's French place does killer food and is certified by the Green Restaurant Association.

MacCallum House

maccallumhouse.com

Chef Alan Kantor is devoted to local, sustainable ingredients and featuring organic wine—and the food he puts out at this Mendocino, California inn is mouth-watering *and* fun. Will and I liked it so much we might have our wedding reception here. The menu and wines will be all organic, of course.

Nopa

nopasf.com

Chefs from other San Francisco restaurants come here late-night because the food (local, seasonal) is so good. The owners are as sustainable as possible, recycling and composting like crazy, using extremely renewable kenaf paper for their menus, and serving filtered tap water instead of bottled.

Theo Chocolate

These chocolate makers craft bars and crazy cute confections from organic, fair trade cocoa beans.

White Dog Café

whitedog.com

This Philly restaurant is passionate about sustainable ingredients, derives its energy from wind power, and gives all food scraps to local pig farmers.

Occasional things

Paporganics

paporganics.com

Sophisticated hemp-and-recycled-paper gift wrap, recycled tissue paper, and ribbon, plus a collection of organic cotton stationery.

Square One Vodka

squareonevodka.com

Vodka fermented from organic American rye.

Viva Terra

vivaterra.com

My favorite ecofriendly home catalog and a great source for dishes, glassware, serving pieces, linens, and more.

Transportation things

Jorg & Olif

jorgandolif.com

These sweet-looking bikes are old-school in appearance but ahead of the curve in design—the perfect combination for a tooling-around ride.

Toyota Prius

toyota.com

The leader in the hybrid car market, the Prius drives great and, of course, rocks on the mileage.

Zipcar

zipcar.com

This car sharing service eliminates the need to own a car in the city. There are BMWs, Mini Coopers, and Priuses in the fleet.

Travel things

70 Park Avenue Hotel

70parkave.com

Green chic in NYC. This Kimpton-owned hotel was designed by Jeffrey Bilhuber.

Driving Green

drivinggreen.com

Offset car travel, flights, or the transportation emissions from everyone coming to an event.

Hotel Green

vanessanoelhotelgreen.com

This chic boutique hotel from fashion designer Vanessa Noel is decked out with organic sheets, chemical-free mattresses, and milk-based paints.

Kimpton Hotels

Kimptonhotels.com

With a growing collection of snazzy hotels all over the country— from D.C. to Denver and Salt Lake City to Scottsdale—and Kimpton EarthCare (that is, environmentally friendly practices) in place at all of them, Kimpton is a good go-to whenever you're on the road.

Lake Austin Spa Resort

lakeaustin.com

Among this award-winning destination spa's most noticeable green factors are the local organic ingredients—both on the menu of cuisine and featured in the pampering treatments.

Orchard Garden Hotel

theorchardgardenhotel.com

The greenest hotel in one of the world's greenest cities (that would be San Francisco), the Orchard Garden has a rigorous energy-saving program, in-room recycling, and nifty amenities that will please the pickiest of travelers.

Post Ranch Inn

postranchinn.com

I would like to move in to Post Ranch. I can't afford it, but I'd like to. This little Big Sur hotel combines luxury with quirky architecture (there are tree houses—literally) and incredible respect for nature.

Stowe Mountain Lodge

stowemountainlodge.com

This luxurious new Stowe resort has organic sheets and towels, recycling bins in guest rooms, and a commitment to working with environmentally friendly local artisans—among a host of other green practices.

TerraPass

terrapass.com

A straightforward way to offset carbon emissions by investing in renewable energy programs.

Chapter Eleven

SOURCE STUFF

In the course of researching this book I read a seemingly endless number of books and articles and interviewed dozens of experts in their fields. These are the books I found especially useful and informative, and I recommend them to anyone who wants to delve further into the magical worlds of green living, sustainability, climate change, and consumerism.

An Inconvenient Truth: The Planetary Emergency of Global Warming and What We Can Do About It by Al Gore (Rodale, 2006).

Consumed: How Markets Corrupt Children, Infantilize Adults, and Swallow Citizens Whole by Benjamin R. Barber (Norton, 2007).

Cradle to Cradle: Remaking the Way We Make Things by William McDonough and Michael Braungart (North Point Press, 2002).

Deep Economy: The Wealth of Communities and the Durable Future by Bill McKibben (Times Books, 2007).

Field Notes from a Catastrophe: Man, Nature, and Climate Change by Elizabeth Kolbert (Bloomsbury, 2006).

Garbage Land: On the Secret Trail of Trash by Elizabeth Royte (Back Bay Books, 2005).

The Omnivore's Dilemma: A Natural History of Four Meals by Michael Pollan (The Penguin Press, 2006).

Silent Spring (40th Anniversary Edition) by Rachel Carson (Mariner Books, 2002; first edition, 1962).

Twinkie, Deconstructed: My Journey to Discover How the Ingredients Found in Processed Foods Are Grown, Mined (Yes, Mined), and Manipulated into What America Eats by Steve Ettlinger (Hudson Street Press, 2007).

In addition, the Environmental Protection Agency (epa.gov), the Natural Resources Defense Council (nrdg.org), the Sierra Club (sierraclub.org), the National Audubon Society (Audubon.org), Grist (grist.org), and *National Geographic*'s The Green Guide (thegreenguide.com) are invaluable sources of excellent information.

For those seeking information on more drastic home design changes, check out *Green Remodeling: Changing the World One Room at a time* by David Johnston and Kim Master (New Society Publishers, 2004) and *The Solar House: Passive Heating and Cooling* by Daniel Chiras (Chelsea Green, 2002).

ACKNOWLEDGMENTS

Many, many thanks to:

My agent, Stacey Glick, who went way above and beyond for *Green Chic*—including finalizing the deal from a hospital bed a day after giving birth to her beautiful second daughter, Alea.

My editor, Shana Drehs, who got *Green Chic* from the start, took the subject matter to heart, and offered savvy advice every step of the way.

Whitney Lehman and Christiaan Simmons, two very enthusiastic and sincere publicists.

The friends who gave me green ideas and encouragement along the way, read sections of the manuscript, and offered honest and invaluable feedback—especially Lorin Seidman, one of the chicest green gals I know, who shares my hatred of ketchup and appreciation of local organic vegetables that taste better than doughnuts; Kerri Bowen, the fabulous and brilliant soon-to-be-PhD-in-literature, who told me which phrases in *Green Chic* didn't work "syntactically with the rest of the prose" and whom I adore beyond words; and my brother, Seth Matheson, who is there for me throughout every project and is without a doubt the best brother on the planet.

And most of all, endless thanks and love to Will Adams, who supported this idea from its inception, read chapters at every phase, tried just about everything with me, and encouraged me (in his inimitable way) to go deeper and explain better.

INDEX